THE
HOLLY JOLLY
QUIZ BOOK

THE
HOLLY JOLLY
QUIZ BOOK

HarperCollins*Publishers*
1 London Bridge Street
London SE1 9GF

www.harpercollins.co.uk

First published by HarperCollins*Publishers* 2020

10 9 8 7 6 5 4 3 2

A catalogue record of this book is available from the British Library

ISBN 978-0-00-843420-5

Printed and bound in Great Britain by CPI Group (UK) Ltd, Croydon

MIX
Paper from
responsible sources
FSC **FSC™ C007454**
www.fsc.org

This book is produced from independently certified FSC™ paper to
ensure responsible forest management.

For more information visit: www.harpercollins.co.uk/green

Contents

CONTENTS

CONTENTS

CHAPTER 1

IT'S BEGINNING TO LOOK A LOT LIKE QUIZMAS

How to Have the Ultimate Christmas Quiz Night

So, you've bought this book because you like quizzes, you like Christmas, you like music and films – or simply because you have no idea how to entertain your family or friends this Christmas. Well, whatever your reason, we have you covered, and an epic night of quizzing awaits you.

In case you don't throw quiz nights every week, here are some simple tips so you can craft the ultimate evening and impress everyone with what a smooth operator you are.

The Quiz Master

It is eminently possible to run the night without a quiz master: the answers are all at the back of the book, so anyone can simply read out the questions without knowing the answers and then look them up at the end.

But if you like feeling omniscient and superior to all your friends ('You really thought Owen Wilson was the star of *Elf*??'), you may wish to take on the role of quiz master yourself. It will also keep things running smoothly, add a sense of theatre to the proceedings and help to settle arguments ('Surely I get a half point for knowing that Bing Crosby sang "White Christmas"?' '*No*, the question was who sang "Blue Christmas"!').

To be the quiz master you will need: this book. That's pretty much it. But you could also wear a special outfit (some sort of top hat or similar is always impressive), use a microphone (it doesn't need to work, but it will likely give you more swagger) and maintain zero tolerance for any tomfoolery. As quiz master, what you say goes. You must be fair but strict. It's a great responsibility.

Equipment

To run a successful quiz you will need:
- Paper – a few sheets for each team. If you want to be super-organised, you can print out/write out answer sheets for your teams (Round 1: 1, 2, 3, etc.), but you could always leave that job up to them. For the picture round, you can either photocopy those pages or give each team some time with the book. Another option is to take photos of these pages on your phone and either print them out or send them to the players.
- Pens (make sure they work).
- Prizes (make sure they're good ones).
- Scoreboard (optional).

Choosing teams

Now, you need to try to make this fair. It's no fun without some real competition. Try to split up players from the same generation (Granny may not have seen *The Holiday*, but she's probably watched *Holiday Inn*). You can choose your own team sizes, as this will obviously depend on how many players you have – but around four is a nice number. You may also wish to consider how your teams can sit comfortably in the space you have, and whether they are able to confer without talking so loudly that the other teams can steal their answers …

Rules

1. One point is awarded for every correct answer. Half points are awarded at the discretion of the quiz master.
2. No cheating.
3. No phone use during quiz time (partly to enforce Rule 1, but also because it's antisocial).
4. Whatever the quiz master says goes. And whatever answer this book says is right is the answer (even if some know-it-all wants to dispute it. Entertain that sort of behaviour and you'll have anarchy on your hands).

Timing

You can decide how fast/slow to run your quiz, but try to keep things relatively pacey or people will get bored, and maintain a pleasant spirit of merry competition throughout. If time allows, why not spread your quiz out over the festive period to fill slow moments?

If you don't have time to do every round of the quiz, pick the ones that are most likely to appeal to those present. The key is to have fun, so make use of this book and adapt it to your needs. Just make sure you allow time at the end to give out prizes – or what has it all been for?

Note: The questions in this section are all multiple choice, but if you want to make things harder you can always just read the question and not the possible answers. Be aware that some questions ask which of the answers is NOT correct, so in those instances you will need to read out all the possible answers.

ROCKIN' ROBIN:
MUSIC

ROUND 1

OFFICIAL CHRISTMAS NUMBER ONES

ROUND 1: OFFICIAL CHRISTMAS NUMBER ONES

1. Which band or artist holds the record for the most
    Christmas number ones ever, with four?

    Bing Crosby
    The Beatles
    Cliff Richard
    Nat King Cole

2. Robbie Williams topped the UK singles chart in
    2001 with a cover of 'Somethin' Stupid', sung with
    which actress?

    Dolly Parton
    Kate Winslet
    Holly Valance
    Nicole Kidman

3. Cliff Richard reached the UK Christmas number one
    in 1988 with which song?

    'Little Drummer Boy'
    'Mistletoe and Wine'
    'Saviour's Day'
    'Merry Christmas Everyone'

4. What song was the 2019 Christmas number one?

    'I Love Sausage Rolls' by LadBaby
    'Own It' by Stormzy ft. Ed Sheeran and
        Burna Boy
    'Before You Go' by Lewis Capaldi
    'Don't Start Now' by Dua Lipa

5. In Band Aid's 1984 version of 'Do They Know
   it's Christmas?', who sang the lyrics 'But say a
   prayer / And pray for the other ones / At
   Christmas time'?

    Boy George
    Paul Young
    Sting
    George Michael

6. Mr Blobby had a surprise number one in 1993, with
   what song?

    'Blobby Blobby Blobby'
    'Mr Blobby'
    'A Blobby Christmas'
    'Pink Snowballs'

7. Which of these songs was the only one to be a Christmas number one?

   'I Wish It Could Be Christmas Everyday' by Wizzard (1973)
   'Lonely This Christmas' by Mud (1974)
   'Last Christmas' by Wham! (1984)
   'Fairytale of New York' by the Pogues and Kirsty MacColl (1987)

8. Who was the first *X Factor* winner to top the Christmas charts?

   Alexandra Burke
   Leon Jackson
   Leona Lewis
   Shayne Ward

9. Which pop group achieved three consecutive Christmas number ones in the Nineties?

   The Spice Girls
   Westlife
   East 17
   Take That

10. Boney M. achieved a Christmas number one
with 'Mary's Boy Child' in 1978, but which artist
first took it to the top of the Christmas chart
in 1957?

Harry Belafonte
Dickie Valentine
Conway Twitty
Elvis Presley

11. In the sixty-six years that a Christmas number
one has been recorded, how many have been
about Christmas?

Five
Twelve
Eighteen
Twenty-three

12. Three choirs have achieved Christmas
number ones – which of the following is NOT one
of them?

St Winifred's School Choir
The Military Wives
Christ Church Cathedral Choir, Oxford
The Lewisham and Greenwich NHS Choir

13. What song did Ed Sheeran have a Christmas number one with in 2017?

    'Perfect'
    'Sing'
    'Shape of You'
    'Beautiful People'

14. An online campaign catapulted what band to the number-one spot for Christmas in 2009?

    JLS
    Rage Against the Machine
    One Direction
    The Darkness

15. What band achieved the Christmas number one twice with the same song – the only band in the history of the UK singles chart to have done so?

    The Beatles with 'I Want to Hold Your Hand'
    Slade with 'Merry Xmas Everybody'
    Wings with 'Mull of Kintyre'
    Queen with 'Bohemian Rhapsody'

(See page 188 for the answers.)

ROUND 2

FAVOURITE CHRISTMAS HITS

1. Who had a huge hit in 1935 with a song
    called '*Stille Nacht, heilige Nacht*' in Germa...
    remains the fourth-bestselling single of all ti...

    Nat King Cole
    Bing Crosby
    Frank Sinatra
    Peter Andre

2. Which of the following artists HASN'T covered
    Mariah Carey's classic 'All I Want for Christmas
    Is You'?

    John Mayer
    Shania Twain
    Demi Lovato
    Britney Spears

3. In 1953, Eartha Kitt had the biggest hit of her career
    with what song?

    'I Saw Mommy Kissing Santa Claus'
    'Santa Baby'
    'Rockin' Around the Christmas Tree'
    'Santa Claus Is Comin' to Town'

4. In 1946, Nat King Cole recorded a hit with a song about 'chestnuts roasting on an open fire'. What is the name of this song?

   'The Christmas Song'
   'Merry Christmas To You'
   'Yuletide Joy'
   'Make the Season Bright'

5. Which singer had a hit in 1970 with 'Feliz Navidad'?

   Julio Iglesias
   José Feliciano
   Juan Gabriel
   Perry Como

6. What is listed in *Guinness World Records* as not only the bestselling Christmas song of all time, but the bestselling single overall, with 50 million estimated sales?

   'All I Want for Christmas Is You' (1994)
   'White Christmas' (1942)
   'Rudolph the Red-nosed Reindeer' (1939)
   'Do They Know It's Christmas?' (1984)

7. Who released the 2011 album *Under the Mistl...*

   Michael Bublé
   Shania Twain
   Justin Bieber
   Cee Lo

8. 'I Believe in Christmas' was a surprise hit by which children's TV act in 2001?

   The Tweenies
   The Teletubbies
   The Chuckle Brothers
   Bob the Builder

9. In 2019, John Legend sang a politically correct version of 'Baby, It's Cold Outside' with which other singer?

   Kelly Clarkson
   Chrissy Teigen
   Gwen Stefani
   Alicia Keys

10. What did Destiny's Child receive on the eighth day of Christmas in 1999?

    A gift certificate to get my favourite CDs
    The keys to a CLK Mercedes
    A pair of Chloé shades and a diamond belly ring
    A crop jacket and dirty denim jeans

11. Chris Rea released his classic 'Driving Home for Christmas' in what year?

    1968
    1978
    1988
    1998

12. About which 1979 song were the following words written: 'Love it or hate it, few songs within the McCartney oeuvre have provoked such strong reactions.'

    'Mull of Kintyre'
    'Wonderful Christmastime'
    'Christmas Time (Is Here Again)'
    'Happy Xmas (War Is Over)'

13. What is the second part of the title of The Darkness's 2003 hit 'Christmas Time'?

'(Don't Let the Bells End)'
'(Feigning Joy and Surprise)'
'(A Snowflake's Hope in Hell)'
'(Come On, Kids)'

14. Shakin' Stevens had a runaway success with his single 'Merry Christmas Everyone' in 1985. What country does the singer come from?

Sweden
Wales
USA
Germany

15. After the release of 'Last Christmas' by Wham! in 1984, George Michael was sued for plagiarism by the writers of which Barry Manilow hit?

'Could It Be Magic'
'Mandy'
'I Write the Songs'
'Can't Smile Without You'

(See page 188 for the answers.)

ROUND 3

SONGS FROM THE MOVIES

ROUND 3: SONGS FROM THE MOVIES

1. Which Christmassy song plays at the end of the 1988
    film *Die Hard*?

    'Let It Snow! Let It Snow! Let It Snow!'
    'All I Want for Christmas (Is My Two Front Teeth)'
    'Santa Claus is Comin' to Town'
    'Rockin' Around the Christmas Tree'

2. In the film *Elf* (2003), what song did the crowd sing
    to keep Santa's sleigh airborne?

    'Rudolph the Red-nosed Reindeer'
    'Jingle Bells'
    'Santa Claus Is Comin' to Town'
    'Here Comes Santa Claus'

3. What song was originally written for the 1944 classic
    Meet Me in St. Louis, to be sung by Judy Garland to
    cheer up her sister after she goes on a middle-of-the-
    night, snowman-destroying rampage?

    'Frosty the Snowman'
    'Have Yourself a Merry Little Christmas'
    'Winter Wonderland'
    'It Came Upon the Midnight Clear'

4. Which film ends with all the characters breaking into a spontaneous performance of 'Put a Little Love in Your Heart'?

   Jingle All the Way (1996)
   The Family Man (2000)
   Bad Santa (2003)
   Scrooged (1988)

5. What song does Kermit the Frog, in the character of Bob Cratchit, sing in *The Muppet Christmas Carol* (1992) as he closes up for Christmas?

   'One More Sleep 'til Christmas'
   'There's Magic in the Air'
   'Merry Christmas to All'
   ''Tis the Season to Be Jolly'

6. What song does Hugh Grant's prime minister character carol-sing with his driver in *Love Actually* (2003)?

   'O Christmas Tree'
   'The Holly and the Ivy'
   'We Three Kings'
   'Good King Wenceslas'

7. Which *X Factor* winner had a Christmas number one
   in 2007 with their version of 'When You Believe'
   from *The Prince of Egypt*?

Leon Jackson
Leona Lewis
Alexandra Burke
Shayne Ward

8. In *The Nightmare Before Christmas* (1993), what song
   does Jack sing as he explores Christmas Town for the
   first time?

'Kidnap the Sandy Claws'
'I Can't Believe My Eyes'
'This Is Christmas'
'What's This?'

9. What song do the Plastics perform in skimpy
   Christmas dresses in their school talent show in *Mean
   Girls* (2004)?

'A Holly Jolly Christmas'
'Jingle Bell Rock'
'I Saw Mommy Kissing Santa Claus'
'Santa Baby'

10. Dolly Parton's Christmas hit 'Hard Candy Christmas' was from which of her films?

    A Country Christmas Story (2013)
    The Best Little Whorehouse in Texas (1982)
    Steel Magnolias (1989)
    A Smoky Mountain Christmas (1986)

11. John Williams and Leslie Bricusse earned an Academy Award nomination for the original song 'Somewhere in My Memory', the signature tune for which film?

    Miracle on 34th Street (1994)
    Santa Claus: The Movie (1985)
    Home Alone (1990)
    Serendipity (2001)

12. What film did Bing Crosby's massive hit 'White Christmas' originally appear in?

    Christmas in Connecticut (1945)
    Holiday Inn (1942)
    It Happened on Fifth Avenue (1947)
    White Christmas (1954)

13. In *About a Boy* (2002), Hugh Grant's ci
    off the royalties of a song written by his
    Name that song, is it:

    'Santa's Super Sleigh'
    'Ho Ho Ho'
    'Look Who's Coming Round the Bend!'
    'The Happiest Elf in Christmasland'

14. Which Christmas film ends with all the characters
    gathered around a tree, singing 'Auld Lang Syne'?

    It's a Wonderful Life (1946)
    A Christmas Carol (2009)
    The Shop Around the Corner (1940)
    Jack Frost (1998)

15. What Christmas classic became the soundtrack of
    nightmares for Billy's mum in *Gremlins* (1984)?

    'Silent Night'
    'Little Drummer Boy'
    'God Bless the Child'
    'Do You Hear What I Hear?'

(See page 189 for the answers.)

ROUND 4

CHRISTMAS CAROLS

ROUND 4: CHRISTMAS CAROLS

1. 'Carol of the Bells', popularised in part due to its appearance in the film *Home Alone* (1990), was originally written in which language?

    Ukrainian
    Dutch
    Romanian
    Italian

2. How many verses are there in 'Away in a Manger'?

    Two
    Three
    Four
    Five

3. What is the poor man doing in 'Good King Wenceslas'?

    Gathering firewood
    Knocking on the door
    Weeping
    Sitting with his head in his hands

4. In what year was 'Silent Night' first performed?

   1518
   1618
   1718
   1818

5. In 'A Christmas Carol', the 2010 *Doctor Who* Christmas special, what song does Katherine Jenkins (in the role of Abigail) sing to calm the floating shark?

   'In the Bleak Midwinter'
   'Once in Royal David's City'
   'Ding Dong Merrily on High'
   'O Little Town of Bethlehem'

6. The tune of 'Greensleeves' is used for which of these carols?

   'Sussex Carol'
   'What Child Is This?'
   'O Come, O Come, Emmanuel'
   'The Holly and the Ivy'

7. In the 'Coventry Carol', what does Herod order his men to do?

   Kill baby Jesus
   Collect taxes
   Build a tower of gold
   Slay all the babies

8. 'Jingle Bells' was originally written for which holiday?

   Halloween
   Thanksgiving
   Kwanzaa
   New Year

9. What historical event inspired 'Do You Hear What I Hear?'

   The American Civil War
   The Cuban Missile Crisis
   The Vietnam War
   The Great Depression

10. Which Christmas carol, often appearing in nativity plays, has been recorded by Gracie Fields, Vera Lynn, Aled Jones and The Beverley Sisters, among others?

'Little Donkey'
'Away in a Manger'
'The Virgin Mary Had a Baby Boy'
'I Heard the Bells on Christmas Day'

11. Who are the lyrics to 'Away in a Manger' most often attributed to?

Martin Luther
Thomas Cromwell
Thomas Tallis
Anne Boleyn

12. Which song was sung by German, English and French troops during the famous Christmas truce of the First World War in 1914?

'It Came Upon the Midnight Clear'
'The First Noel'
'Silent Night'
'The Holly and the Ivy'

13. Who released a version of 'Joy to the
turning it into a massive hit?

Sonny & Cher
Curved Air
David Cassidy
Three Dog Night

14. In which carol do the angels sing 'Peace on the Earth,
goodwill to men / From Heaven's all-gracious King'?

'I Heard the Bells on Christmas Day'
'We Three Kings'
'While Shepherds Watched Their Flocks'
'It Came Upon the Midnight Clear'

15. Which of these carols is the oldest?

'We Three Kings'
'God Rest Ye Merry, Gentlemen'
'O Come, O Come, Emmanuel'
'O Little Town of Bethlehem'

(See page 190 for the answers.)

ROUND 5

GUESS THE SONG FROM THE LYRIC

ROUND 5: GUESS THE SONG FROM THE LYRIC

1. 'You gotta believe me, you just gotta believe me /
   Come on, fellas, believe me, you just gotta believe me'

2. 'My god, I thought you were someone to rely on'

3. 'I won't make a list and send it to the North Pole for
   Saint Nick / I won't even stay awake to hear those
   magic reindeer click'

4. 'Said Santa to a boy child, "What have you been
   longing for?"'

5. 'Fall on your knees / Oh hear the angel voices'

6. 'I wanna wish you a Merry Christmas / From the bottom of my heart'

7. 'I sing this song / To pass the time away'

8. 'O tidings of comfort and joy'

God rest ye merry gentlemen

9. 'Oh, ho, the mistletoe / Hung where you can

10. 'Hang a shining star upon the highest bough'

11. 'I want a yacht and really that's not a lot / Been an angel all year'

12. 'Mistletoe hung where you can see / Every couple tries to stop'

13. 'Dub-a-dub-a-dum-dum / Dub-a-dub-a-dum / Dub-a-dum-dum-dub-a-dum / Dub-a-dub-a-dum'

14. 'I don't wanna miss out on the holiday / But I can't stop staring at your face'

15. 'I signed my letter that I sealed with a kiss / I sent it off and just said this, "I know exactly what I want this year"'

16. 'The playing of the merry organ / Sweet singing in the choir'

The Holly & the Ivy

17. 'If you jump into your bed / Quickly cov
    head'

18. '"Fear not," said he, for mighty dread / Had seized
    their troubled mind; / "Glad tidings of great joy I
    bring / To you and all mankind"'

19. 'And the only things I see / Are emptiness and
    loneliness / And an unlit Christmas tree'

20. 'But the prettiest sight to see is the holly that will be /
    On your own front door'

(See page 190 for the answers.)

ROUND 6

FIND THE LINK

In this round, answer each of the five questions and work out what song links the answers. An adjudicator should read out the questions below with a fifteen-second interval between them. As soon as any player thinks they have worked out the link they should shout out the answer – but if they are wrong, they will not be allowed to guess again. Another member of their team is still allowed to guess, however.

For each link that is guessed correctly, five points should be awarded.

What Christmas song links the answers to these five questions?

- Newspaper with adult content on page three.
- Bambi.
- TV series, starring Claire Foy and Olivia Coleman in the same role.
- Poisonous DC supervillain.
- Fearne's best friend, who presents *This Morning*.

What Christmas song links the answers to these five questions?

- What the band The Prodigy liked to start.
- Vorderman plus King plus Ann Duffy.
- 1998 film starring Michael Keaton as a snowman.
- Pinocchio's one got bigger.
- Conker tree.

What Christmas song links the answers to these five questions?

- The postman does it twice.
- Which Billie wants to?
- Keith Moon, Ringo Starr, Phil Collins.
- Duck Duck _____
- Robin's Marian.

What Christmas song links the answers to these five questions?

- Name of the son in *The Incredibles* (2004).
  Also a hyphen.
- Why Bing Crosby goes to Vermont.
- Hidalgo, Pilgrim or Shadowfax.
- _____ *in Your Lane*, bestselling book in 2018.
- Hand, cow, church, bicycle, door.

(See page 191 for the answers.)

ROCKIN' ROBIN: PICTURE ROUND

Dingbats Merrily on High

Identify the Christmas song in the following puzzles:

1.

2.

3.

4.

5.

6.

7.

8.

9.

10.

11.

12.

(See page 191 for the answers.)

Match the Artist to the Song

Draw a line to reunite these Christmas bangers with their singer.

Ariana Grande   'My Sad Christmas Song'

Bon Jovi   'I Saw Mommy Kissing Santa Claus'

The Jackson 5   'Please Come Home for Christmas'

Kanye West   'Step Into Christmas'

Miley Cyrus   'Underneath the Tree'

Leona Lewis   'Christmas in Harlem'

Elton John   'One More Sleep'

Kelly Clarkson   'Wit It This Christmas'

(See page 192 for the answers.)

ROCKIN' ROBIN: PICTURE ROUND

Festive Music Scramble!

Unscramble the letters to discover the name of a favourite Christmas song.

ENTITLED YOLK

HYDRA SYMBOLIC

A EARLIER TOFFY WONKY

GOBLIN CELL JERK

DUNNO HURL PURR

DEB REMOTE THIRTY MULL

(See page 192 for the answers.)

ROCKIN' ROBIN: FOR KIDS (AND BIG KIDS)

Festive Music Quiz

1. In the song 'The Twelve Days of Christmas' what is
    given on the tenth day?

    Lords a-leaping
    Geese a-laying
    Maids a-milking
    Ladies dancing

2. What is another name for the song '*O Tannenbaum*'?

    'O Merry Christmas'
    'O Christmas Tree'
    'O Come, All Ye Faithful'
    'O Come, O Come, Emmanuel'

3. How many 'las' are there in the first verse of 'Deck
    the Halls'?

    Eight
    Sixteen
    Twenty-four
    Thirty-two

4. What wouldn't the other reindeer let Rudolph do?

Play games
Pull the sleigh
Laugh
Sleep in the shed

5. What is Frosty the Snowman's nose?

A carrot
A lump of coal
A wooden spoon
A button

6. When Santa got stuck up the chimney, where does he say he had soot?

In his beard
In his sack
In his boots
In his hat

7. In 'Away in a Manger', what woke up the baby Jesus?

The cows mooing
The arrival of the wise men
Mary tickling him
Knocking on the door

8. In the song 'I Saw Mommy Kissing Santa Claus', where did this event take place?

On the stairs
Under the mistletoe
On the sofa
In the kitchen

9. In ''Twas the Night Before Christmas', what does St Nicholas exclaim in the last line?

'To bed, to bed, for it shall soon be Christmas morn!'
'A very Merry Christmas, to one and all!'
'Until next year, peace and love to each of you!'
'Happy Christmas to all, and to all a good night!'

10. In the song 'Santa Claus Is Comin' to Town', how many times does Santa check his list?

✓ Twice
Thrice
He gets the reindeer to check it
He doesn't need to check it

11. In the song 'Winter Wonderland', the singer wants to build a snowman and pretend he is ...?

The sharpest dresser in town
Parson Brown
Wearing a crown
Doctor Frown

12. What would you famously 'deck the halls' with?

Strings of mistletoe
✓ Boughs of holly
Paperchains
Baubles

13. Which one of these characters will 'go down in history'?

Frosty the Snowman
Rudolph the Red-nosed Reindeer
Mrs Claus
Mr Grinch

14. In the song 'We Wish You a Merry Christmas', what's important about the figgy pudding?

That it's really nice
That they have some
That there is lots of it
That it's hot

15. In the song 'Little Donkey', what is the donkey carrying?

A dusty load
An endless load
A heavy load
A precious load

(See page 193 for the answers.)

QUIZ ACTUALLY: MOVIES

4. Which of the following is considered a classic Christmas film, set in a luxury townhouse that a drifter is squatting in?

It Happened on 5th Avenue (1947)
Singin' in the Rain (1952)
Rear Window (1952)
Manhattan (1979)

5. *Scrooge* (1970), starring Albert Finney, won an Academy Award for which original song?

'I Like Life'
'Thank You Very Much'
'I'd Do Anything'
'Consider Yourself'

6. Cary Grant and Loretta Young starred in a classic 1947 film about whose wife?

The Professor's
The Bishop's
The Shopkeeper's
The Headmaster's

7. What is the name of the small town in which *It's a Wonderful Life* (1946) is set?

    Bedford Falls
    Pleasantville
    Springwood
    Magnolia Springs

8. Who wrote the music for *Holiday Inn* (1942), with twelve new songs composed specifically for the film?

    Irving Berlin
    Rodgers and Hammerstein
    Stephen Sondheim
    Andrew Lloyd Webber

9. In 1978, ITV started their long-running tradition of airing a Bond film in the middle of prime time on Christmas Day. What 1971 film was the first to air?

    Dr. No
    Diamonds Are Forever
    The Living Daylights
    GoldenEye

10. Which 1948 western starring John Wayne is a
retelling of the nativity story?

Lone Star
Once Upon a Time in the West
The Salvation
3 Godfathers

11. In *White Christmas* (1954), song-and-dance duo
Wallace and Davis put on a show to help a ski-lodge
owner. But what relation is he to them?

Their old school headmaster
Their army general from the war
Their grandfather
The director who gave them their first big break

12. *Scrooge* (1951) is widely considered to be the most
definitive film version of *A Christmas Carol*, and the
most faithful to the original. Which of the below does
the Ghost of Christmas Yet to Come NOT show
Scrooge?

The Cratchit family mourning Tiny Tim
His own grave
His maid stealing his belongings
A former employee in the poor house

13. The earliest Christmas film ever made is believed to be *Santa Claus*, a short silent British drama, directed by George Albert Smith. What year was it made?

1898
1910
1921
1933

14. What is the name of the 1974 festive slasher film featuring a group of sorority sisters who are stalked by a deranged killer, which became a surprise Christmas hit?

Black Christmas
The Long Night
Christmas at the Lake House
While I Was Watching

15. According to lists in Rotten Tomatoes, the *Independent*, *Esquire*, Thrillist, *Time Out* and the *Standard* (among many others), what is the greatest Christmas film of all time?

   Miracle on 34th Street (1947)
   Home Alone (1990)
   It's a Wonderful Life (1946)
   White Christmas (1954)

(See page 193 for the answers.)

ROUND 2

THE GOLDEN AGE – A MILLENNIAL'S CHILDHOOD

1. What is the highest-grossing Christmas film, having taken an estimated $477 million?

   The Muppet Christmas Carol (1992)
   Home Alone (1990)
   Miracle on 34th Street (1994)
   How the Grinch Stole Christmas (2000)

2. What is Jack Skellington's dog called in *The Nightmare Before Christmas* (1993)?

   Six
   Zero
   Bones
   Oogie Boogie

3. Which Christmas movie features a cameo from Donald Trump?

   Scrooged (1988)
   Home Alone 2: Lost in New York (1992)
   Die Hard (1988)
   Trading Places (1983)

4. In *Die Hard* (1988), what does John McClane write on a terrorist's sweater to send a message to Hans Gruber?

Welcome to the party, pal
Yippee-ki-yay
Now I have a machine gun. HO - HO - HO
You throw quite a party!

5. Who played Ebenezer Scrooge in *The Muppet Christmas Carol* (1992)?

Michael Caine
Patrick Stewart
Anthony Hopkins
Kermit the Frog

6. In the 1983 Christmas comedy *Trading Places*, how much does Randolph bet Mortimer that he can make common criminal Billy Ray Valentine a successful businessman?

$1,000,000
$1
$100
$1,000

7. Who directed *Gremlins* (1984) as well as *Home Alone* (1990) and *Home Alone 2: Lost in New York* (1992)?

John Landis
Robert Zemeckis
Steven Spielberg
Chris Columbus

8. What terrible fate befalls Santa Claus when he visits Scott Calvin's home at the start of the hit 1994 film *The Santa Clause*?

He falls from his sleigh in the sky
He gets stuck in a chimney
He chokes on milk and cookies
He falls off the roof

9. What is the name of the 'hottest-selling toy' in the 1996 blockbuster film *Jingle All the Way*?

Atomic-Man
Laser-Kid
Turbo-Man
Power Ranger

10. In *About A Boy* (2002), which one of these gifts does Marcus NOT receive for Christmas?

A CD player
Socks
Tambourine
Trainers

11. Where has the Grinch been living for fifty-three years when he decides to steal Christmas in *How the Grinch Stole Christmas* (2000)?

Mount Crumpit
Mount Whoville
Mount Grump
Mount Grouchy

12. In the 1988 film *Scrooged*, what form does the Ghost of Christmas Past take?

A taxi driver
A fairy
A homeless man
A television executive

13. What was the name of the department store in the 1994 film *Miracle on 34th Street*?

    Macy's
    Cole's
    Gimbel's
    Kringle's

14. In *Home Alone 2: Lost in New York* (1992), what have Harry and Marv changed their criminal name to?

    The Wet Bandits
    The Sticky Bandits
    The Slime Bandits
    The Toy Bandits

15. Which of these romantic comedies does NOT begin at Christmas?

    While You Were Sleeping (1995)
    You've Got Mail (1998)
    Serendipity (2001)
    Sleepless in Seattle (1993)

(See page 194 for the answers.)

ROUND 3

A MORE MODERN CHRISTMAS

1. Which Netflix holiday film is set in the fictional country of Aldovia?

    The Knight Before Christmas (2019)
    A Christmas Prince (2017)
    Holiday in the Wild (2019)
    The Christmas Chronicles (2018)

2. In *Elf* (2003), the four main food groups for Elves are 'candy, candy canes, candy corns and –' what else?

    Syrup
    Chocolate
    Marshmallows
    Candy floss

3. In *The Holiday* (2006), what is Amanda unable to do until the end of the movie?

    Celebrate Christmas
    Quit her job
    Laugh
    Cry

4. What is on Mark Darcy's ugly Christmas jumper when Bridget first meets him at her mum's annual turkey curry buffet in *Bridget Jones's Diary* (2001)?

A robin
A snowman
A turkey
A reindeer

5. How many films have there been in the *Nativity!* film series?

Two
Four
Five
Three

6. In *The Night Before* (2015), what is the exclusive Christmas Eve party that Ethan, Isaac and Chris are trying to find?

The Jingle Ball
The Gingerbread Ball
The Mistletoe Ball
The Nutcracker Ball

7. Which actor stars opposite Reese Witherspoon in *Four Christmases* (2008)?

Vince Vaughn
Owen Wilson
Ben Stiller
Jason Bateman

8. In the 2003 romcom *Love Actually*, Natalie tells Prime Minister David that she lives in the dodgy end of which neighbourhood?

Hackney
Wandsworth
Tower Hamlets
Croydon

9. In *The Family Stone* (2005), what ingredient does Meredith accidentally put in her Christmas strata that Everett is allergic to?

Mushrooms
Eggs
Onion
Milk

10. Which actress does NOT star in the 2017 comedy *A Bad Moms Christmas*?

    Jada Pinkett Smith
    Kristen Bell
    Kathryn Hahn
    Susan Sarandon

11. What gift does Thurman want from Santa in *Bad Santa* (2003)?

    An Xbox
    A pink elephant
    Friends
    An iPod

12. Who makes a cameo alongside her then-fiancé Ryan Reynolds in the 2005 Christmas rom-com *Just Friends*?

    Blake Lively
    Scarlett Johansson
    Alanis Morissette
    Sandra Bullock

13. Who did Emma Thompson co-write the story with on which the 2019 film *Last Christmas* is based – eight years prior to the movie's release?

Andrew Ridgeley
Greg Wise
Richard Curtis
George Michael

14. How many of the eight movies in the *Harry Potter* film franchise include a Christmas scene?

Eight
Six
Four
Five

15. What was the most-rented DVD in the UK in 2004?

Love Actually
Elf
The Polar Express
The Holiday

(See page 195 for the answers.)

ROUND 4

CRITICS' REVIEWS – IDENTIFY THE FILM

1. About which 1990 movie was it written: 'This slapstick is vicious; a family film?'

2. 'Ahnold terminates the holiday spirit.' Which critically pummelled 1996 film received this damning review?

3. 'Cloying fancy gives way to gross-out comedy, twisted social commentary, affecting pathos, and weirdly sexualized romance in this lurid live-action version of the classic children's book.' Which 2000 film does this describe?

4. 'A different angle is taken for the legal case in this movie and it works quite well in creating a fairytale miracle within the middle of corporate America.' Which 1994 film is being described here?

5. 'With a little tweaking, this could be a horror film.'
   Which beloved 2003 Christmas film received this
   caustic review?

6. 'In a year of Bad Moms, Bad Santas and Bad
   Neighbours, this is essentially Bad Employees:
   another irresponsible-adults comedy, another great
   cast, and another erratic script.' Which 2016
   Christmas comedy does this describe?

7. 'I like to think if […] some spirit could have taken
   [Dickens] into the future to show him the adaptations
   to come, this is the one he would have especially
   favoured.' Which adaptation of *A Christmas Carol* is
   this review praising?

8. 'You'd be hard-pressed to find another movie –
   holiday or otherwise – that makes the case so
   convincingly for how miserable the lives of women
   truly are, and how all fired up awesome it is to be a
   man. A manly man who loves tea. And that's one big
   holiday lump of sexist coal that stinks, actually.'
   Which 2003 movie is being described here?

9. 'Watching it is like unwrapping an attractively packed gift only to discover it's socks again.' Which star-packed, festive rom-com favourite of 2006 is being described here?

10. 'Yikes – Santa dies!' Which 1994 children's film got this stunned review?

11. 'A Wonderful title for a motion picture about which practically everyone who sees it will agree that it's wonderful entertainment.' What Christmas film was being reviewed here in 1946?

12. 'The music of George Michael and Wham! is hauled out on to the soundtrack of this mouldy tangerine of a movie with about the same level of care and sensitivity that you might find on the festive mixtape at a motorway service station.' Which 2019 box-office hit is being described here?

13. 'A subversive parable on the dangers of irresponsible pet care that doubles as an antidote to small-town Americana and Yuletide sentimentality.' Which 1984 movie is being summarised here?

14. About which 2003 black comedy was this written: 'Made with the Scrooges of the world in mind. Generally, if you love Christmas, this isn't going to be your cup of tea. But if you hate the Yuletide season, you're part of the target audience.'

15. '[A] pathetic comedy about a no-hope primary school, which [...] becomes convinced that Hollywood casting agents are coming to this year's nativity play. Even in outline, the plot wouldn't pass muster as an episode of a CBBC drama.' Which hugely popular 2009 Brit flick is being reviewed here?

(See page 195 for the answers.)

ROUND 5

GUESS THE FILM FROM JUST ONE QUOTE

ROUND 5: GUESS THE FILM FROM JUST ONE QUOTE

1. 'Every time a bell rings, an angel gets his wings.'

2. 'I am Colin, God of Sex. I'm just on the wrong continent, that's all.'

3. 'I'm sorry I ruined your lives and crammed eleven cookies into the VCR.'

4. 'I'm gonna kill that kid.'

5. 'Since I am dead, I can take off my head to recite Shakespearean quotations.'

6. 'I'm not just a whimsical figure who wears a charming suit and affects a jolly demeanour, you know. I'm a symbol.'

7. 'I'm not a pervert! I was just looking for a Turbo-Man doll!'

8. 'Vermont must be beautiful this time of year ... all that snow!'

9. 'You're Rudolph, a freak with a red nose. Nobody likes you.'

10. 'Boy that's scary stuff! Should we be worried about the kids in the audience?'

11. 'Oh Christmas isn't just a day, it's a frame of mind.'

12. 'It's too early. I never eat December snowflakes. I always wait until January.'

13. 'No, you're a hallucination, brought on by alcohol. Russian vodka, poisoned by Chernobyl.'

14. 'Tell the birds I said goodbye.'

15. 'I've seen this before! Sleigh fever, they call it! The pressure of Christmas sends a man doo-lellied-tap! Santa Claus XVI of 1802! Every child that year got a sausage nailed to a piece of bark!'

(See page 196 for the answers.)

ROUND 6

FIND THE LINK

In this round, answer each of the five questions and work out what film links the answers. An adjudicator should read out the questions below with a fifteen-second interval between them. As soon as any player thinks they have worked out the link they should shout out the answer – but if they are wrong, they will not be allowed to guess again. Another member from their team is still allowed to guess, however.

For each link that is guessed correctly, five points should be awarded.

1. What Christmas film links these five answers?

- Boys who had a hit with 'Little Saint Nick' in 1964.
- Everybody's waiting for the man with it.
- Arthur Christmas's relationship to Santa.
- Where Kevin's mum was when she realised he was missing.
- Ealing Studios 1949 comedy film, _____ *to Pimlico*.

2. What Christmas film links these five answers?

- *Holiday* _____, 1942 film starring Bing Crosby.
- Surname of comedian Ernie.
- Spandau Ballet's best-known hit.
- What is born, according to the 2018 film starring Lady Gaga?
- Shrek's sidekick.

3. What Christmas film links these five answers?

- Comedic actor who performed in the 2012 London Olympics opening ceremony.
- Actor who rose to fame playing Tim Canterbury.
- British actress who has written two books adapted from *The Tale of Peter Rabbit*.
- Singer whose 2000 single 'I'm Over You' charted at number two.
- He has a very specific set of skills. And he will find you. And he will kill you.

4. What Christmas film links these five answers?

- Amy March falls through this, to be rescued by Jo.
- Vixen and Comet.
- Paul Daniels was good at this.
- Wanted someone to love.
- 32°F.

(See page 196 for the answers.)

QUIZ ACTUALLY: PICTURE ROUND

Dingbats Merrily on High

Identify the Christmas film in the following puzzles:

1.

2. ABCDEFG HIJKMNOP QRSTUV WXYZ

3.

4. ~~Sisters~~   ~~Uncles~~

~~Sons~~   **Friends**   ~~Kids~~

~~Teachers~~   ~~Lovers~~

5.

6.

CHRISTMAS

CHRISTMAS   **CHRISTMAS**

CHRISTMAS

7.

8.

9.

10.

11.

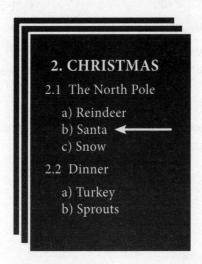

12.

(See page 197 for the answers.)

Blink and You'd Miss Them!

Match the stars to the films they appeared in …

Ant and Dec	*The Night Before*
Steven Tyler (Aerosmith)	*The Holiday*
Alan Carr	*Last Christmas*
Mindy Kaling	*Home Alone*
Dustin Hoffman	*The Polar Express*
Sue Perkins	*Elf*
Peter Dinklage	*Love Actually*
John Candy	*Nativity!*

(See page 197 for the answers.)

Festive Movie Scramble!

Unscramble the letters to discover the name of a favourite Christmas film.

WHAMS NET ON

RAD HIDE

A MR WHISK THATCHER STINK

AN SAD BAT

YEAH HOLD IT

COG SORE

(See page 198 for the answers.)

QUIZ ACTUALLY: FOR KIDS

Festive Movie Quiz

1. What is the name of the snowman in *Frozen* (2013)?

    Olaf
    Marshmallow
    Sven
    Kristoff

2. What drink is served to children on the train in
    The Polar Express (2004)?

    Tea
    Chocolate milk
    Eggnog
    Hot chocolate

3. In *Arthur Christmas* (2011), how does Santa travel
    around the world?

    A hovercraft
    A sleigh pulled by reindeers
    A private jet
    A hot air balloon

4. What colour is the Grinch in *The Grinch* (2018)?

   Blue
   Red
   Green
   Yellow

5. Where does Jack Skellington live in *The Nightmare Before Christmas* (1993)?

   Christmas Town
   Halloween Town
   Easter Town
   Scary Town

6. What is the name of the funny classroom assistant who appears in the *Nativity!* film series?

   Mr Poppy
   Mr Tulip
   Mr Daisy
   Mr Rose

7. In *The Nutcracker and the Four Realms* (2018), what is Clara searching for in the magical land of the Four Realms?

   A magical mirror
   Chocolate
   The Sugar Plum Fairy
   The key to her mother's music box

8. What creature is Manny in the *Ice Age* films?

   A sabre-toothed cat
   A sloth
   A mammoth
   An opossum

9. In *The Snowman* (1982), what does the little boy have to remember the Snowman by at the end of the film?

   A hat
   The snow
   A scarf
   A carrot

10. In *A Christmas Carol* (2009), how many ghosts visit
    Ebenezer Scrooge?

    Two
    Three
    Ten
    Four

11. In *The Christmas Chronicles* (2018), what does Santa
    Claus tell Teddy and Kate that he doesn't say?

    Peace and joy to everyone
    Let it snow!
    Merry Christmas
    HO HO HO

12. What does Andy get as a present for Christmas at the
    end of *Toy Story* (1995)?

    Buzz Lightyear
    A puppy
    A cat
    Little Bo-Peep

13. In *Stick Man* (2015), where does Stick Man live with his Stick Lady Love and his three Stick Children?

    The Family Tree
    The Family Bush
    The Family Stick-house
    The Family Shrub

14. In *The Star* (2017), what gifts do the three camels, Felix, Cyrus and Deborah, bring for the baby Jesus?

    Gold, frankincense and a manger
    Gold, frankincense and money
    Gold, frankincense and merry
    Gold, frankincense and myrrh

15. In *The Grinch* (2018), which of the following things did the Grinch NOT steal from Whoville?

    The Christmas decorations
    The presents
    Cindy Lou Who
    A sleigh

(See page 198 for the answers.)

CHAPTER 2

THE TWELVE GAMES OF CHRISTMAS: FUN FOR ALL THE FAMILY

Introduction: How to Make Your Teams

Fantastic! You've decided to make Christmas Day and the festive season THAT MUCH MORE FUN by playing some games!

If everyone can handle a touch more merriment, you can make the team selection a little game, too.

Decide on the size of the teams beforehand, then assign a Christmas carol to each team (one you're sure everyone will know well). Write down the name of each Christmas carol on slips of paper, so that there will be one for each team member.

You can then either hand these out arbitrarily so that the team members are selected randomly, or select your teams in advance and ensure that every member of each team gets the same one.

As one, all players present must start humming their carol and walking around the room until they have found everyone else humming the same carol as them. When they have found their entire team, they must join hands and sing the rest of the carol LOUDLY. The first team to do this wins!

CHRISTMAS SING-SONG MASH-UP

Warning: this game is pretty hard!

For this game you will need a timer, two small bags, some slips of paper and some pens. Divide into equal teams.

Before playing the game, write down on slips of paper the names of Christmas carols to be put into one bag, and the names of Christmas pop songs to put into the other bag. They should be pretty well-known ones. Allow a couple of each per player.

Work out whose name comes first alphabetically out of everyone present. That will be the team to go first, and that player must start.

The starting player should take one piece of paper out of each of the bags. They must sing the words of the pop song to the tune of the Christmas carol (for example, the lyrics of 'All I Want for Christmas Is You' to the tune of 'Away in a Manger'), and their team must guess what the carol is. A timer should be set for one minute. If their team does not guess it, discard the papers and move on to the next team.

If they do, they should retain the slip of paper with the carol's name on it.

When every player present has had a turn, count up the slips to determine which team has the most papers. That team has won and should be suitably lauded.

SANTA'S LAP

This isn't a competitive game, so you don't need to divide into teams, but it's a great ice breaker! You will need slips of paper, pens and a bag. A Santa costume is highly recommended, but not necessary.

Start off by writing the names of characters from Christmas films on slips of paper and placing them in a bag. There are suggestions for good characters you could choose on the next page, but you can of course pick your own favourites.

Select one player to be 'Santa'. They will be the guesser.

Everyone else should take a slip of paper from the bag, being careful not to show anyone else. That will be the character they need to play.

Everyone should then take their turn in Santa's grotto, with the other players forming the audience. Santa will talk to each one in turn, asking them yes or no questions to try to discover their identity. There is one exception to this rule: he can ask what they want for Christmas. They must respond in character, using any physical cues or accents to give a clue.

If Santa can't guess, see if the other players have worked it out!

Note: A fun extension of this game is to play it over Christmas dinner, when players have to stay in character until they have been guessed!

Suggested Characters

Buddy the Elf, from *Elf*
Kevin McCallister, from *Home Alone*
Jack Skellington, from *The Nightmare Before Christmas*
Billy Mack, from *Love Actually*
Clarence Odbody, from *It's a Wonderful Life*
The Ghost of Christmas Present, from *A Christmas Carol*
Bob Cratchit (aka Kermit the Frog), from *The Muppet Christmas Carol*
Amanda Woods, from *The Holiday*
Mr Poppy, from *Nativity!*
Kris Kringle, from *Miracle on 34th Street*
Hans Gruber, from *Die Hard*
Howard Langston, from *Jingle All the Way*
The Central Park Pigeon Lady, from *Home Alone 2: Lost in New York*
Jack Frost, from (you guessed it) *Jack Frost*
The Grinch, from *The Grinch Who Stole Christmas*
Beth March, from *Little Women*
Grandsanta, from *Arthur Christmas*

Jacob Marley's ghost (aka Goofy), from *Mickey's Christmas Carol*

Olaf, from *Frozen*

The Snowman, from *The Snowman* (note: no words allowed. Shaking or nodding the head must suffice.)

FESTIVE GUESS THAT SKETCH: TWO WAYS

1. *Traditional Guess That Sketch*

For this game you will a need a timer, notecards and either a large pad of paper for each team or several sheets. Divide into teams.

A judge (or someone who is not playing) should write out individual words on the notecards that each fall into one of these categories:

Films
Songs
Person, Place, Animal
Action
Object

You can either colour-code the cards or write the category initials (F, S, PPA, etc.) in the top corner of the card. You should also mark every fifth card with AP (All Play).

There are some word suggestions over the page, but you can also be creative and come up with your own –

but they should all be related to Christmas films or songs.

Decide which team goes first, and who from that team will draw in the first round. They must draw the word on each card on the large pad or sheets of paper for their team to guess. The judge prepares a timer (thirty seconds to make it a little harder, or one minute), and signals for that person to start. If their team is able to guess the word in the allotted time, they receive a point for their team and can take another turn. If not, it's the next team's turn.

If it's an All Play card, all teams must compete against each other. Whoever wins steals the point, but play continues as before.

Keep playing until the cards run out, or the turkey/nut roast is ready!

Note: If you prefer, all the players can contribute answers.

Rules

The artist cannot write any letters or numbers.
The artist can't make any noises or gestures.

Possible word ideas
Films

Miracle on 34th Street
Holiday Inn
Frozen **AP**
Deck the Halls
The Nutcracker Prince

Die Hard
Arthur Christmas
Four Christmases
The Polar Express
The Nightmare Before Christmas
Little Women **AP**
Home Alone 2: Lost in New York

Songs

'The Little Drummer Boy'
'I Saw Mommy Kissing Santa Claus'
'Last Christmas'
'Mistletoe' **AP**
'We Wish You a Merry Christmas'
'Rockin' Around the Christmas Tree'
'Happy Xmas (War Is Over)'
'Mary's Boy Child'
'I Saw Three Ships (Come Sailing In)' **AP**
'Don't Shoot Me Santa'
'Santa Claus Is Comin' to Town'
'While Shepherds Watched Their Flocks'

Person, Place, Animal

Scrooge
The North Pole
The Grinch
The Snowdog

FESTIVE GUESS THAT SKETCH: TWO WAYS

London **AP**
The Ghost of Christmas Past
George Michael
Winter Wonderland
New York **AP**
Rudolph the Red-nosed Reindeer
Elvis
The airport

Action

Ringing	Bring
Dash	Kiss **AP**
Laugh **AP**	Toasting
Play	Carolling **AP**
Rocking	Hiding
Dancing	Jingle

Object

Sleigh	Mall
Carrot **AP**	Ivy
Shop	Cottage
Maple syrup	Night
Airplane **AP**	Manger
Knight	King

2. *Guess that Sketch With a Twist*

If energy levels are high, this twist on the traditional drawing game is great fun.

You will need a judge for this one, who will sit in a central point in the house. They will have a list of all the words that will appear in the game – around twenty, not divided into categories but random.

When they shout 'Go!' one player from every team should approach the judge, who will whisper the first word to them. They must quickly run back to their team and draw it for them. Whoever guesses it must run to the judge and tell them the answer, to be given the next word. This is repeated until one of the teams finishes the entire list, and shouts 'IT'S CHRIIIISSSTMAAAS!' to signal their victory.

Note: Teams should avoid shouting out the answers to the judge, thus giving the other teams an advantage. If possible, it is best to put teams in different rooms to help prevent overhearing.

WHO AM I?
(THE POST-IT GAME)

For this game you will need a stack of Post-it Notes and a pen. It can be played any time but is a great one for in between courses at Christmas dinner.

Everyone takes a Post-it and writes a name on it. You can decide whether to keep this to fictional Christmas characters, actors or artists who have recorded a Christmas song – or all of the above. (You will find some name ideas on the following page.) Each player then sticks that Post-it onto the head of the person to their left.

The youngest player goes first: they ask everyone a yes or no question about who they are, i.e. 'Am I older than fifty?' 'Am I female?' If they receive a 'yes' answer, they can proceed to ask more questions until they get a 'no'. At that point, the turn passes to the player on their left, and continues around the circle.

Whoever guesses their person first (they will need to wait until their turn and ask, 'Am I X?' as one of their questions) is the winner, but play continues until everyone has identified who they are.

Name Ideas

Hugh Grant
Beth March
Leona Lewis
Richard Attenborough
John Lennon
Sandy Claws
Amanda Seyfried
Kirsten Dunst
Billy Mack
Bing Crosby
Tom Hanks
The Turbo-Man Doll
Mariah Carey
Victor Landberg of Shopper's Express

NAME THAT TUNE

You do not need to divide into teams to play this game. You can use an instrument, but it is not essential.

You will need to pick someone to either play notes on an instrument or to hum them. They will be the adjudicator and should decide on a few Christmas songs that they will be testing the players with.

The players should then challenge each other as to how many notes they will need to hear before they can guess what the song is. For instance, one may say ten notes, so another may go one better and predict they can guess it in nine.

Once every player has staked their number, the adjudicator will play or hum the lowest number of notes staked. That player will then have the opportunity to guess what the tune is. If they're unable to, the adjudicator will play/hum it again with the additional number of notes that the next player has staked, and on until someone can guess it correctly. That player will win a point for the round.

You can play as many rounds as you like and vary the adjudicator if desired.

Ideas for Songs

'Wonderful Christmastime'
'Merry Christmas Everyone'
'Good King Wenceslas'
'Mary's Boy Child'
'O Come, All Ye Faithful'
'Holly Jolly Christmas'
'All I Want for Christmas Is You'
'O Little Town of Bethlehem'
'Lonely This Christmas'
'Jingle Bells'
'Fairytale of New York'
'Have Yourself a Merry Little Christmas'
'Joy to the World'
'We Three Kings'
'Baby, It's Cold Outside'

SGNOS (BACKWARDS SONGS)

You will need one person to act as the host. Everyone else should divide up into two teams. You will need some sort of buzzer for each side. Sleigh bells are acceptable.

The host should call up one player from each team to stand on either size of the 'buzzer'. The host will then sing a line from a Christmas song backwards, slowly. The first player to guess the song should press the buzzer (or equivalent) and sing the line back to the host the right way round. This will win them a point for their team. Two more players should then come up and take their turn – continue playing for as long as you like!

Below are some ideas you could use (a mixture of pop songs and carols), but of course you can make up your own, too.

Ideas

Tonight sleigh my guide you won't, bright so nose your
    with Rudolph. ('Rudolph, the Red-nosed Reindeer')
Sleigh horse-one a in gliding go to, time swell a is time bell
    Jingle. ('Jingle Bell Rock')

Dismay you nothing let, gentlemen, merry ye rest God. ('God Rest Ye Merry, Gentlemen')

Teeth front two my is, Christmas for want I all. ('All I Want for Christmas Is My Two Front Teeth')

Shed-cattle lowly a stood, City David's Royal in once. ('Once in Royal David's City')

Ringing are bells the heav'n in, high on merrily! Dong Ding. ('Ding Dong Merrily on High')

White snowy so beard his underneath, Claus Santa tickle Mommy saw I. ('I Saw Mommy Kissing Santa Claus')

'Jolly be let's', singing voices, hear you when feeling sentimental a get will you. ('Rockin' Around the Christmas Tree')

Ground the on seated all, night by flocks their watched shepherds while. ('While Shepherds Watched Their Flocks')

Glistening is snow, lane the in. ('Winter Wonderland')

Delightful so is fire the but, frightful is outside weather the oh. ('Let It Snow!')

Jolly to be season the 'tis, la-la-la-la, la-la-la-la-fa. ('Deck the Halls')

Birds calling four: me to gave love true my. ('The Twelve Days of Christmas')

Pum pump um rum pa, bring we gifts finest our. ('The Little Drummer Boy')

Listen children and, glisten treetops the where. ('White Christmas')

Peace heavenly in sleep, mild and tender so infant holy. ('Silent Night')

Exultation in sing, angels of choirs, sing O. ('O Come, All Ye Faithful')

Afar traverse we gifts bearing, are Orient of kings three
we. ('We Three Kings')

Pout not better, cry not better you, out watch better you.
('Santa Claus Is Comin' to Town')

Hay the on asleep Jesus lord little the, lay he where down
looked sky bright the in stars the. ('Away in a Manger')

Day Christmas of because evermore for live will man and,
Day Christmas on born was Christ Jesus child boy
Mary's. ('Mary's Boy Child')

Kin your and you to, bring we tidings good. ('We Wish
You a Merry Christmas')

Stephen of feast the on, out looked Wenceslas King Good.
('Good King Wenceslas')

Nose button a and pipe corncob a with, soul happy jolly a
was Snowman the Frosty. ('Frosty the Snowman')

CAROL BINGO

For this game, every player needs a pen and a piece of paper. You will also need a timer.

For each round, a word (commonly found in Christmas songs) should be called out by a judge at the same time as the timer is started. You can decide how long it's set for by the age of the players, but around a minute is recommended. All players then have until the timer goes off to list on their piece of paper every song they can think of containing that word. (Google may be a useful tool for settling any disputes over song lyrics.)

Every correct answer scores the player a point for that round. You can play as many rounds as you like!

Ideas for Words

Santa	Year
Snow	Christmas
Time	Know
Baby	Good
Bells	

CHRISTMAS CATEGORIES

For this game, every player will need a piece of paper and a pen. They will also need to be able to see a list of the ten categories; you can either write them up on a large board or give everyone their own little list written out. You will also need a means of generating a random letter – you may have a spinner, you could use an app or simply stab a newspaper at random with a pencil and whatever it lands on is your letter.

In advance of playing the game, you need to decide what the categories will be. There are some suggested on the next page, but you can swap in your own.

You will need someone to call a letter and start the timer, but they can still join in and play. From when the letter is called, players have three minutes to write down an answer in each of the categories – all beginning with the chosen letter.

When the time is up, players take it in turns to read out their answer for the first category. Any player who has a unique answer receives a point, but if there are any duplicates, a point is not awarded. Continue to read out answers for all the categories.

You can continue to play as many rounds as you like for as long as people are interested!

Ideas for Categories

Films that might be on TV around Christmas
Words in a Christmas song
Something you would eat at Christmas
Shops in which you might buy a present
Girl's name/boy's name that might be on Santa's list
Countries that Santa will visit
Things that are red
Things you might receive as a present
Things made of wood
Surnames of actors (male or female) who have appeared in
  a Christmas film

WHO'S THAT IN SANTA'S BAG?

You will need a timer, a bag, some slips of paper and pens. Decorating the bag with some tinsel or similar will certainly add to the fun but it is not obligatory.

Each player should write down on slips of paper the names of people, either real or fictional, related to Christmas films or songs (see pages 130 and 131 for ideas). These should be placed in the bag. Depending on how long you wish to play for, you can decide how many slips each player should put in the bag, but between five and ten each is recommended. Try to ensure that all the names are famous enough to be known by at least half of the players.

Divide the players up into two equal teams.

Time to play!

Round 1 (describing):

One team goes first, and they should nominate a player to start. The timer is set for one minute, during which that player should pick names out of the bag one by one and describe them – as many as they can in the time. They can only pass once, and cannot say what that word rhymes with, forbidden words in another language or any of the letters in that person's name. Once the minute is up, that player retains the slips guessed correctly and puts any unguessed slips back in the bag. Play then passes to the other team. This continues with a different player each time, until there are no slips left. Keep a note of how many slips each team has won, and then place them all back in the bag.

Round 2 (acting):

Repeat what you did in Round 1, but this time speaking no words. You can do anything you like as long as it's non-verbal. Once again, keep playing until there are no slips left and take a note of how many each team has won. Then place them all back in the bag.

Round 3 (one word):

In this round, players are only allowed to use one word. You may not act anything out or try to sneak in any extra words.

When you have finished playing, add your scores from each round together to determine the winner!

CHRISTMAS FILM AND SONG-TITLE CHARADES

This is classic charades but made all the more festive with Christmas categories! You just need a timer, some slips of paper and a pen.

Someone will need to write out the names of Christmas films or songs on slips of paper. Then simply divide up into teams and take it in turns to act out the answers. You can decide how long to give teams to guess – somewhere in the region of one minute.

Common clues that you can use:

- Pretend to crank a camera to indicate a film and pretend to sing into a microphone for a song. If it's also a book, you can put your hands together and open them like you're reading.
- To indicate the number of words in the title, hold up that many fingers. When describing each word, you can then indicate the number of the word you're describing.

- If breaking up the word into syllables, hold that number of fingers against your arm.
- If you want to suggest that the word sounds like another, pull on your ear.
- If someone has guessed part of the charade correctly, point one index finger to your nose and the other to that person.
- For a longer version of someone's answer, pretend to stretch out elastic. If shorter, mime a karate chop.

Below are some suggestions that would be fun to act out!

Songs

'Rockin' Around the Christmas Tree'
'All I Want for Christmas Is My Two Front Teeth'
'Little Donkey'
'Step Into Christmas'
'Frosty the Snowman'
'Rudolph, the Red-nosed Reindeer'
'Silent Night'
'Sleigh Ride'
'The Little Drummer Boy'
'I Saw Mommy Kissing Santa Claus'
'Fairytale of New York'
'Let It Snow!'
'I Saw Three Ships'

CHRISTMAS FILM AND SONG-TITLE CHARADES

Films

The Nutcracker and the Four Realms
You've Got Mail
The Lion, the Witch and the Wardrobe
The Shop Around the Corner
Die Hard
Bad Santa
Gremlins
How the Grinch Stole Christmas
The Nightmare Before Christmas
Frozen
The Snowman and the Snowdog
The Polar Express
Trading Places

CHRISTMAS SONG SWITCH-UPS

For this game, you will need song sheets prepared beforehand. These can be printed or written song lyrics to a few Christmas songs (one for each of the players) with at least one random word missing from each line. Below the blank space, you should indicate if the missing word should be an object, place, person, exclamation, verb or adjective. You will also need to provide a pen for each of the players.

Hand out a song sheet to everyone present, then go round the room and allow each player to request a word in whatever category they need from a player of their choice, without giving any information as to the context. For example: 'Aunty Sal, may I have the name of a person, please?' Aunty Sal should then think of a random name – for example, Tinkerbell, Elvis or Boris Johnson – and the player should then fill the blank space with this answer.

Continue going round the room in circles, until everyone has a completed song. At this point, each player reads their new and 'improved' song aloud. Or, if they are feeling brave, singing it is definitely encouraged. Hilarity will almost certainly ensue.

A completed verse should look something like this:

Oh, the weather outside is <u>IMPERTINENT</u>
ADJECTIVE

But the <u>LETTUCE</u> is so delightful
OBJECT

And since we've no place to <u>EXPLODE</u>
VERB

Let it <u>MEDICATE</u>, let it <u>SPLATTER</u>, let it <u>BURP</u>
VERB   VERB   VERB

ACT IT OUT

For this game, it can be fun to provide props and costumes (a random selection of whatever you have lying around), but this is by no means crucial.

Divide up into teams – these don't need to be equal, as long as you have a couple of players in each willing to take starring roles. Each team should decide on a Christmas film and scene they wish to portray. They will be miming it for the other teams (no words allowed) so it should be a physical one! Allow a few minutes for each team to decide on their scene and practise in different rooms before showtime.

Teams will then take it in turns to act out their scene for the others, while audience members (the other teams) must try to guess what the film is that they're portraying. You could have prizes for whoever guesses it first to fuel the competitive spirit!

Teams are likely to wish to decide on their own scenes, but here are some suggestions.

Scene Ideas

The finale of *It's a Wonderful Life*

The mailroom scene in *Elf*

Any number of violent scenes from *Home Alone* (due caution advised)

'Keep the change, ya filthy animal,' from *Home Alone 2: Lost in New York*

'Sisters, Sisters', in *White Christmas*

Hans Gruber's fall in *Die Hard* (another one to be careful with!)

The courtroom scene in *Miracle on 34th Street*

'Jingle Bell Rock' from *Mean Girls*

CHAPTER 3

IT'S THE MOST WONDERFUL TIME FOR A BEER: FUN FOR ADULTS ONLY

Introduction: A Caution, and Non-drinking Alternative Penalties

While it is certainly possible for adults to play games from the family section, the games in this section are strictly for adults only. They are either filthy or involve liquor. Or both.

It seems only right to offer a caution here: we do not advocate heavy drinking at any time of year, and certainly not at Christmas. Inebriation is only more likely to cause the ever-dreaded family arguments. But, assuming everyone present will play responsibly, drinking games can be a hell of a lot of fun. Just make sure no one is playing with straight vodka, and that Uncle Bill, who can't hold his liquor, either has a non-alcoholic beer for every second drink or watered-down gin with a lot of tonic.

However, if you have guests that are staying sober this Christmas, you may wish to decide upon alternatives to drinking penalties. You can get creative with these and personalise them to your guests, but here are some suggestions:

- **Edible punishment**. Perhaps whoever loses must eat a Brussels sprout for every game they lose? A tablespoon of bread pudding? Or something spicy like a spoonful of lime pickle or Tabasco?
- **Chores**. The loser must clear the table/do the washing up/serve up dessert for everyone before they're allowed to have theirs.
- **Physical humiliation**. Ten press-ups for the loser?

- **Play the troll**. Perhaps the loser has to sit the next round out under the table?

The other option is to keep the penalties as drinking ones, but some guests simply have non-alcoholic drinks. If this is what you opt for, something fizzy will help to make this a little more difficult for them. Where's the fun in water?

AT THE DINNER TABLE

You may find that the dinner is enough to keep everyone entertained (it's hard to argue with a faceful of roast potatoes), but if you wish to fill the gaps between courses, or everyone is too full to move afterwards, these are some great games to help add some fun.

INCOGNITO SONG TITLES

This game can run throughout Christmas dinner, as it's best played when the other players' guards are down. The aim is to casually slip the title of a Christmas song into conversation, without anyone noticing. Think –

'I'm so glad to have all the family together. MERRY CHRISTMAS EVERYONE!'

'I'm going to call my grandparents this evening. I do wonder – DO THEY KNOW IT'S CHRISTMAS?'

'I love Christmas pudding. Did we have it LAST CHRISTMAS?'

If no one notices, everyone around the table must drink. If someone spots it, you must finish your drink.

It seems only fair to have different levels to this game, as some song titles are going to be much harder to slip into conversation than others. 'Last Christmas' would be pretty easy (perhaps everyone takes a large sip), but if you manage to get 'God Rest Ye Merry, Gentlemen' in there, I think you're going to have to insist that they all finish their drinks.

EROTIC TITLES

This is another game that you could have running throughout the meal.

As your guests sit down, challenge them to come up with a funny, erotic version of a classic festive film, and allow this to percolate while they eat their dinner. After the main course, everyone must write their answer down and put it into a hat (keeping them anonymous).

You then read them aloud, one by one, and everyone must vote on which is the best. Perhaps a pack of jellied willies for the winner?

Non-Christmas Porno Titles for Inspiration

The Devil Wears Nada
Romancing the Bone
Good Will Humping
Indiana Bones and the Temple of Poon

Inspect-Her Gadget
Throbbin' Hood
The Loin King
Grinding Nemo
Saturday Night Beaver
Womb Raider
Lord of the G-strings

SH*G, MARRY, AVOID: FESTIVE FILM EDITION

This game is a great conversation starter, and the perfect way to fill any quiet moments (perhaps if dinner ends up being several hours later than planned). The concept is very simple – someone suggests three Christmas film characters, and the others have to choose which of them they would sh*g, marry or avoid. You can let your guests come up with suggestions for the three people (and no need to stick to just one gender for each round!), but let's get the ball rolling.

Ideas for Questions

Love Actually (take 1) – Karl (Rodrigo Santoro), Jamie (Colin Firth), Peter (Chiwetel Ejiofor)
Love Actually (take 2) – Billy Mack (Bill Nighy), the Prime Minister (Hugh Grant), Daniel (Liam Neeson)
Love Actually (take 3) – Juliet (Keira Knightley), Carla 'the real friendly one' (Denise Richards), Carol (Claudia Schiffer)
Love Actually (take 4) – Natalie (Martine

143

McCutcheon), Karen (Emma Thompson), Jeannie
(January Jones)

Sexy Santas – Kris Kringle from *Miracle on 34th Street*
(Richard Attenborough, the 1994 version), Santa in *The
Christmas Chronicles* (Kurt Russell), Scott Calvin in
The Santa Clause (Tim Allen)

Elf – Buddy (Will Ferrell), his dad (James Caan), Miles
Filch (Peter Dinklage)

The Holiday (the gals)– Amanda (Cameron Diaz), Iris
(Kate Winslet), Lindsay Lohan (herself)

The Holiday (the guys) – Graham (Jude Law), Miles
(Jack Black), Jasper (Rufus Sewell)

Little Women – Jo March (Winona Ryder, the 1994
version), Mrs March (Susan Sarandon, the 1994
version), Meg March (Emma Watson, the 2019 version)

A Bad Moms Christmas – Amy (Mila Kunis), Kiki (Kristen
Bell), Carla (Kathryn Hahn)

Home Alone – Harry (Joe Pesci), Marv (Daniel Stern), Gus
Polinski (John Candy)

The Family Stone – Meredith (Sarah Jessica Parker), Amy
(Rachel McAdams), Julie (Claire Danes)

Classic leading ladies – Kathleen Kelly from *You've Got
Mail* (Meg Ryan), Esther Smith from *Meet Me in
St. Louis* (Judy Garland), Kate from *Four Christmases*
(Reese Witherspoon)

Action-film hotties – John McClane from *Die Hard* (Bruce
Willis), Howard Langston from *Jingle All the Way*
(Arnold Schwarzenegger), Martin Riggs from *Lethal
Weapon* (Mel Gibson)

ROUND THE FIRESIDE

Post dinner is the time when guests start to get sleepy and you could easily lose the rest of the day. Inject some more energy into proceedings with these decidedly non-child-friendly games.

NAUGHTY OR NICE SWITCH-UPS

Please refer to page 132 of this book to find the rules for Switch-ups. The adult version is very simple – it's exactly the same, except all the words you offer need to be pure filth. This book will not be giving examples of the sorts of things we'd suggest (this is a family-friendly gift, after all), but if you're not immediately thinking of them now, maybe this game isn't for you anyway …

Note: Choose very carefully whether you want to play this using Christmas carols or not. You may cause great offence to some of your guests.

BACK TO BACK

You may know this as Mr & Mrs or similar, but this is the game in which two players have to stand back to back and answer 'Most likely to'-style questions on scenarios from Christmas films. You can either make paddles that say ME and THEM, and get them to hold up their answer, or if that's too much admin, give them a drink and tell them to take a sip if they believe they're the most likely party. If they disagree on who the most likely person is, they have to drink again!

Here are some possible scenarios you can use, but once again you can invent many of your own.

Most likely to be a stunt-double for a porn film (like John and Judy in *Love Actually*)

Most likely to add maple syrup to their food (like Buddy in *Elf*)

Most likely to give up working ever again if they could live on the royalties of their dad's song (like Will in *About a Boy*)

Most likely to secretly still believe in Santa (like everyone at the end of *Miracle on 34th Street*)

Most likely to get so pissed off with the other person that they burn their most prized possession (like Amy does to Jo in *Little Women*)

Most likely to go on holiday and leave their child behind (like Kevin's parents in *Home Alone*)

Most likely to impress at karaoke (like the boys in *The Night Before*)

Most likely to get fired for throwing an *Office Christmas Party* type of shebang

Most likely to lose the plot if Christmas was stolen by the Grinch

Most likely to do a house swap with someone halfway across the world, without telling anybody (like Amanda and Iris in *The Holiday*)

Who has read more books (like bookworm Belle in *Beauty and the Beast: The Enchanted Christmas*)

Most likely to get engaged to someone they met earlier that day (like Anna in *Frozen*)

Most likely to become a squatter (like Aloysius in *It Happened on 5th Avenue*)

Most likely to believe in fate (like John and Sara in *Serendipity*)

Most likely to perform in a Sexy Santa competition (like Ty in *A Bad Moms Christmas*)

CELEBRITY LINKS

This game is really going to test your celebrity knowledge!

The only prep you need to do for this one is to make a little stack of cards with 'PASS' written on them.

To play, someone starts by saying the name of an actor (i.e. Reese Witherspoon). The next person round the circle then has to say the name of another actor who appeared with them in a film or TV series, such as Vince Vaughn (*Four Christmases*). This continues around the circle, with each player linking the last actor to a new name. If you cannot think of anyone, you should drink while you think.

If you are completely at a loss, you must finish your drink. Play then starts again with a new name.

If the link you identify is a Christmas film or TV show, you can pick up a 'PASS' card to use the next time you're stuck for an answer. When you play this card you must return it to the pile, and play then skips to the person next to you.

GREAT MINDS

Every player should be given a stack of Post-its. Take it in turns to ask the group a question inspired by a Christmas film, and everyone should write their answer on one of the Post-its. If you have the same answer as someone else, you win a point. Whoever has the most points at the end wins!

Examples of Questions

You're the new Bad Santa, and you want to make a fast buck by robbing a celebrity. Who do you target?

You're entering the big Christmas baking competition in mythical Belgravia (as in *The Princess Switch*). What is your signature bake?

It's your last night in the big city before you're claimed by serious, dependable adulthood (as in *The Night Before*). What do you do?

After watching *Love Actually*, you're inspired to head to the airport. You can fly anywhere in the world – where do you go?

The Grinch is in your house, intent on stealing Christmas. What element of Christmas do you fight to protect?

Like Kevin McCallister in *Home Alone*, you get left behind by your family and have the house to yourself for a few days. What is the first thing you do?

Like Kevin McCallister in *Home Alone 2: Lost in New York*, you find yourself in New York for the first time all alone and with your dad's credit card (and he's loaded). What's the first thing you do?

You go to Cole's Department Store and there you can ask Santa for any toy in the shop. What do you go for?

As at the end of *White Christmas*, you finally get a whole heap of snow. What's the first thing you want to do?

You visit Kathleen's store in *You've Got Mail*. You can choose any kids' book to take home – what do you go for?

Like Buddy the Elf, you want to take the object of your affection on a date, but you don't really have any money. What date do you plan?

Which Christmas film star would you most like to spend the night with?

Like Chris Brander in *Just Friends*, the last time you saw everyone at your high school was seriously embarrassing. Now, you're going to see them all again. What would you like to say your job is?

Everett in *The Family Stone* is unfortunately allergic to mushrooms. What's the one food in the world that you would HATE to be allergic to?

In *Four Christmases,* Brad and Kate like to go away so they don't have to spend Christmas with their eccentric relatives. Who out of everyone playing the game today is the most barmy?

CHRISTMAS FILM AND MUSIC DRINKING GAMES

Whether you're having a 'quiet' evening in watching a film or powering up for a night out by blasting out a Christmas tune, here are some basic drinking games that will be sure to get the party started. Of course, you can adapt these to your own favourites, but we've covered most of the festive classics that no Christmas season should be without. Just make sure your drinks are tall and weak, or things could definitely get messy …

RUM-RUM-RUM-RUM-RUM: SONGS

'Stay Another Day' by East 17

Drink two fingers every time you hear the word 'Stay'.

'Last Christmas' by Wham!

Half of the group drinks one finger when George Michael says 'I', while the other half drinks when George says 'you'.

'All I Want for Christmas Is You' by Mariah Carey

Sip every time Mariah Carey sings 'Christmas' and chug your drink for as long as Mariah holds the high note at the end of the song.

'Rockin' Robin' by Michael Jackson

Sip your drink every time Michael Jackson mentions a species of bird. (Warning: This is not for the faint-hearted. He does this twenty-five times in the song.)

'Mistletoe' by Justin Bieber

Drink two fingers whenever Justin says 'shawty' and drink one finger when he says 'mistletoe'.

'8 Days of Christmas' by Destiny's Child

Whenever Destiny's Child mention a number, drink the same number of sips.

'It's Beginning to Look a Lot Like Christmas' by Michael Bublé

Drink two fingers whenever Michael Bublé says, 'It's beginning to look a lot like Christmas,' and finish your drink when Michael sings, 'Sure it's Christmas once more,' at the end of the song.

HOLIDAY GIN: FILMS

Love Actually

Drink two fingers every time a character says 'actually'.

Take a sip every time a character says 'Christmas' or you see the countdown to Christmas on screen.

Drink two fingers whenever Sarah's (Laura Linney) mobile phone rings.

Take a sip every time you hear Billy Mack's song 'Christmas Is All Around'.

Drink one finger whenever a character cries.

Finish your drink every time storylines cross over.

Do a shot any time a character wears a turtleneck.

Drink one finger whenever Jamie (Colin Firth) and Aurelia (Lúcia Moniz) are speaking about the same thing but in different languages.

When Harry (Alan Rickman) appears on screen, shout 'SNAPE!' and when Rufus (Rowan Atkinson) appears on screen, shout 'MR BEAN!'. The last person to shout has to finish their drink.

Bad Santa

Take a sip every time a character says 'f★ck'.

Drink one finger every time a character says 'sh★t'.

Drink two fingers every time a character says 'a★s'.

Finish your drink every time a character says 'b★tch'.

Sip your drink whenever Santa drinks.

Do a shot whenever Santa has sex.

Drink two fingers whenever a kid tells Santa what he wants for Christmas.

Drink one finger whenever a character mentions or makes a sandwich.

When Sue (Lauren Graham) appears on screen, shout 'LORELAI GILMORE!' The last person to shout has to finish their drink.

Elf

Sip your drink whenever a character says 'elf' or 'elves'.

Drink two fingers whenever Buddy (Will Ferrell) shouts 'SANTA!' or gets excited about Santa.

Drink one finger whenever Buddy eats sugar.

Do a shot every time Buddy mentions maple syrup or uses the maple syrup from his pocket.

Sip your drink for as long as Buddy or Jovie sing.

Drink one finger every time Papa Elf narrates the story.

Drink two fingers whenever Walter gets angry at Buddy.

Finish your drink when everyone believes in Santa Claus again.

When Miles (Peter Dinklage) appears on screen, shout 'TYRION LANNISTER!' The last person to shout has to finish their drink.

The Holiday

Sip your drink every time a character mentions 'love' or 'the holidays'.

Drink two fingers whenever the exterior of Iris's (Kate Winslet) house, Rosehill Cottage, appears on screen.

Drink one finger and curse the screen whenever Iris's obnoxious ex-boyfriend Jasper (Rufus Sewell) is mentioned or appears.

Finish your drink every time Amanda (Cameron Diaz) imagines her life as a movie trailer.

Drink one finger whenever Amanda's inability to cry is mentioned.

Do a shot when Iris declares, 'You're supposed to be the leading lady in your own life, for God's sake!'

Drink two fingers every time Miles (Jack Black) sings.

Do a shot when Graham (Jude Law) says, 'I have a cow in my backyard.'

Finish your drink when Amanda finally learns to cry.

When Lindsay Lohan appears on screen, shout 'LINDSAY LOHAN!' The last person to shout has to finish their drink.

Home Alone 2: Lost in New York

Sip your drink every time a character mentions Christmas.

Drink one finger whenever a character shouts 'KEVIN!'

Drink two fingers every time Kevin (Macaulay Culkin) uses his Talkboy tape recorder.

Finish your drink when Kevin's mum, Kate (Catherine O'Hara), realises that she's left Kevin.

Drink one finger every time the Pigeon Lady (Brenda Fricker) appears on screen.

Drink two fingers every time Harry and Marv (Joe Pesci and Daniel Stern) get hurt.

Sip your drink every time the hotel staff go to Kevin's room and respond to Johnny's dialogue in the film *Angels with Even Filthier Souls* – mistakenly thinking it's Kevin's father.

Do a shot and shout 'AND A HAPPY NEW YEAR!' to the screen when you hear the line, 'Merry Christmas, ya filthy animal.'

Finish your drink when Kevin is reunited with his mum at the end of the film.

When Donald Trump appears on screen, shout 'FAKE NEWS!' The last person to shout has to finish their drink.

CHAPTER 4

HOME ALONE? PUZZLES TO KEEP YOU ENTERTAINED

JOLLYWORD PUZZLES

(BECAUSE YOU CAN'T HAVE CROSS WORDS AT CHRISTMAS)

1.

JOLLYWORD PUZZLES

ACROSS

1. 'Man ___ the Bag' by Jessie J (2015) *(4)*
5. '___ to the World' by Aretha Franklin (2006) *(3)*
6. '___' by Josh Groban (2004) *(7)*
8. '___ Maria' by Lesley Garrett and Amanda Thompson (1993) *(3)*
10. '___'s Day' by Cliff Richard (1990) *(7)*
11. '___ Crimbo' by Bo' Selecta! (2003) *(6)*
13. 'Must Be ___' by Bob Dylan (2009) *(5)*
14. 'Fairytale of ___' by The Pogues feat. Kirsty MacColl (1987) *(3, 4)*
17. 'Santa, Teach Me to ___' by Debbie & the Darnells (1962) *(5)*
20. '___ More Sleep' by Leona Lewis (2013) *(3)*
21. '___' Around the Christmas Tree' by Brenda Lee (1958) *(6)*
22. 'All I Want for Christmas Is My Two Front ___' by Spike Jones and His City Slickers (1947) *(5)*
25. 'Stop the ___' by Jona Lewie (1978) *(7)*
28. 'It's the Most Wonderful Time of the ___' by Andy Williams (1963) *(4)*

DOWN

2. 'Lonely ___ Christmas' by Mud (1974) *(4)*
3. 'Happy Xmas (War Is ___)' by John Lennon (1971) *(4)*
4. 'Mr ___, the Christmas Poo' by Mr ___ (1999) *(6)*
5. 'I Have Forgiven ___' by Morrissey (2004) *(5)*
6. '___ Christmas' by Elvis Presley (1957) *(4)*
7. 'Have a ___ Christmas' by The ___ Girls (2003) *(6)*
9. '___' by Justin Bieber (2011) *(9)*
11. 'The ___ of Love' by Frankie Goes to Hollywood (1984) *(5)*
12. '___ the Tree' by Kelly Clarkson (2013) *(10)*
15. '___ More Sleep 'Til Christmas' by Kermit the Frog (1992) *(3)*
16. 'Little Saint ___' by The Beach Boys (1964) *(4)*
17. 'Little ___' by The Beverley Sisters (1959) *(6)*
18. '___ Another Day' by East 17 (1994) *(4)*
19. 'Wombling ___ Christmas' by The Wombles (1974) *(5)*
23. 'I'll Be ___ for Christmas' by Bing Crosby (1943) *(4)*
24. 'Merry ___Everybody' by Slade (1973) *(4)*
26. 'Walking in the ___' by Aled Jones (1985) *(3)*
27. '___ Rudolph ___' by Chuck Berry (1958) *(3)*

(See page 199 for the answers.)

2.

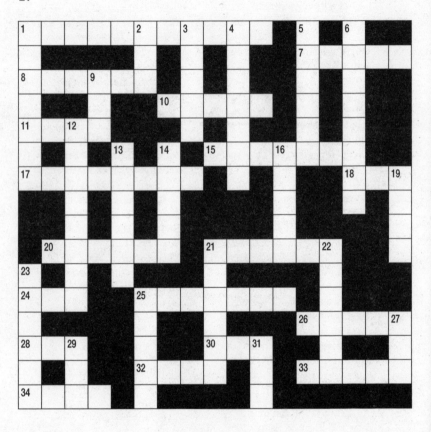

JOLLYWORD PUZZLES

ACROSS

1. ___ (2001), starring John Cusack and Kate Beckinsale *(11)*
7. ___ *IV* (1985), starring Sylvester Stallone *(5)*
8. ___ *Christmas Party* (2016), starring Jason Bateman and Jennifer Aniston *(6)*
10. *Deck the* ___ (2006), starring Matthew Broderick and Danny DeVito *(5)*
11. ___ *Girls* (2004), starring Lindsay Lohan and Rachel McAdams *(4)*
15. *The Snowman and the* ___ (2012), created by Raymond Briggs *(7)*
17. ___! (2009), starring Martin Freeman and Ashley Jensen *(8)*
18. ___ (2003), starring Will Ferrell and Zooey Deschanel *(3)*
20. *The Santa* ___ (1994), starring Tim Allen *(6)*

21. *Christmas with the* ___ (2004), starring Tim Allen and Jamie Lee Curtis *(6)*
24. ___ *Him?* (2016), starring James Franco and Bryan Cranston *(3)*
25. *The* ___ (2006), starring Kate Winslet and Cameron Diaz *(7)*
26. *Beauty and the* ___: *The Enchanted Christmas* (1997), a Walt Disney film *(5)*
28. ___'s *Midnight Garden* (1999), starring Nigel Le Vaillant and Anthony Way *(3)*
30. ___ *to Be Single* (2016), starring Dakota Johnson and Rebel Wilson *(3)*
32. ___ *Christmas* (2019), starring Emilia Clarke and Henry Golding *(4)*
33. *How the Grinch* ___ *Christmas* (2000), starring Jim Carrey *(5)*
34. ___ *Alone* (1990), starring Macaulay Culkin *(4)*

DOWN

1. *The* ___ (1982), a Raymond Briggs film *(7)*
2. ___ *Hard* (1988), starring Bruce Willis and Alan Rickman *(3)*
3. *The* ___ *Express* (2004), starring Tom Hanks *(5)*
4. *Babes In* ___ (1961), starring Ray Bolger and Tommy Sands *(7)*

5. *The Shop* ___ *the Corner* (1940), starring Margaret Sullivan and James Stewart *(6)*
6. ___ (1988), starring Bill Murray *(8)*
9. *Holiday* ___ (1942), starring Bing Crosby and Fred Astaire *(3)*
12. *Love* ___ (2003), starring A LOT of people *(8)*

13. *It Happened on 5th ___* (1947), starring Don DeFore and Ann Harding *(6)*

14. *The Family ___* (2005), starring Sarah Jessica Parker and Diane Keaton *(5)*

16. *Little ___* (1994), starring Winona Ryder and Kirsten Dunst *(5)*

19. *___ Claus* (2007), starring Vince Vaughn and Elizabeth Banks *(4)*

21. *The ___ Before Christmas* (2019), starring Vanessa Hudgens and Josh Whitehouse *(6)*

22. *Miracle on 34th ___* (1994), starring Richard Attenborough and Elizabeth Perkins *(6)*

23. *The Princess ___* (2018), starring Vanessa Hudgens and Sam Palladio *(6)*

25. *Shrek the ___* (2007), starring Mike Myers and Eddie Murphy *(5)*

27. *___ Bishop's Wife* (1947), starring Cary Grant and Loretta Young *(3)*

29. *A Bad ___s Christmas* (2017), starring Mila Kunis and Kristen Bell *(3)*

31. *Jingle All the ___* (1996), starring Arnold Schwarzenegger *(3)*

(See page 200 for the answers.)

3.

ACROSS

1. Surname of the star of *Jingle All the Way* (1996) *(14)*
7. Merry instrument being played in 'The Holly and the Ivy' *(5)*
8. Kate Winslet's character in *The Holiday* (2006) *(4)*
9. 'The best way to spread Christmas _____, is singing loud for all to hear!' *(5)*
10. It's noiseless *(5)*
12. The red man has what sort of allergy in *Santa Claws* (2014)? *(3)*
14. *The _____ and the Four Realms* (2018) *(10)*
16. *Trading Places* (1983) is centred around one of these *(3)*
17. Tiny Tim's relation to Bob Cratchit *(3)*
19. First word in the last verse of 'Hark! The Herald Angels Sing' *(4)*
20. The tunnel Buddy the Elf has to go through *(7)*
23. Most frequently appearing syllable in 'Deck the Halls' *(2)*
24. _____ *a Boy* (2002) *(5)*
25. Mistletoe and what? *(4)*
27. First song ever broadcast from space *(6, 5)*
28. Is *Die Hard* (1988) a Christmas film? *(3)*
29. The famous Louis, who brought his friends together for one of the most celebrated Christmas albums of all time *(9)*

DOWN

1. Hung with care on the night before Christmas *(9)*
2. Swapped in *The Holiday* (2006) *(5)*
3. The shape of a tree-ornament hiding place in *A Christmas Prince* (2017) *(5)*
4. The decade that produced *The Nightmare Before Christmas* and *The Santa Clause* *(8)*
5. The thief of Christmas *(6)*
6. Merry Gentlemen should do this *(4)*
11. Iconic song, also by the 'Merry Xmas (War Is Over)' artist *(7)*
13. American band that has released a brand-new Christmas song every year since 2006 *(3, 7)*
15. Number of lords a-leaping *(3)*
18. Frosty's eyes *(4)*
20. Rejected by Jo March *(6)*
21. The day when Harry and Sally confess their love *(3, 4)*
22. Stacy owns one of these in Chicago in *The Princess Switch* (2018) *(6)*
26. 'Dance of the Sugar ___ Fairies' *(4)*

(See page 201 for the answers.)

4.

ACROSS

1. *Die Hard*'s (1988) city setting *(3, 7)*
7. An unusual place for a boy to be walking in *(3)*
9. Holy, tender and mild *(6)*
10. Mythical being, star of *Shrek the Halls* (2007) *(4)*
11. The Grinch's dog *(3)*
12. The nationality of two embittered lovers in New York *(5)*
13. The Jones who released a Christmas album with Russell Watson in 2019 *(4)*
14. Where Raymond Briggs's Father Christmas racks up a huge hotel bill *(3, 5)*
17. Technology used to create a Christmas song in 2016, described as the 'stuff of nightmares' *(2)*
18. The country that banned carols between 1647 and 1660 *(7)*
19. An activity Chris Rea likes engaging in *(7)*
21. Famous Dudley, star of *Santa Claus: The Movie* (1985) *(5)*
22. 'The Truth Sent From ____', sometimes referred to as the 'Shropshire Carol' *(5)*
23. *Everyday Is Christmas*, an album from which Australian singer-songwriter? *(3)*
26. McClane moves around a tower building in one of these *(4)*
27. Tom Jones sang 'Baby, It's Cold Outside' with this famous Cerys *(8)*
30. Sam, a muppet, was this type of bird *(5)*
31. The state Santa was in, causing him to shout *(5)*
33. Sound made while dashing over the hills in a one-horse open sleigh *(2)*
34. Singer who made a guest appearance in *The Night Before* (2015) *(5, 5)*
36. Santa will find out if you've been this, when he comes to town *(4)*
38. Star of *A Merry Friggin' Christmas* (2014), the actor's final film role *(5, 8)*
42. Animal that appears to a young girl in the Raymond Briggs film of the same name *(4)*

DOWN

1. Singer with only one more sleep to wait *(5, 5)*
2. The fictional kingdom Elsa rules over *(9)*
3. American Christmas horror film, based on the book by Roald Dahl *(8)*
4. The spell Harry would use if he needed light *(5)*

5. The number of parts voiced by Tom Hanks in *The Polar Express* (2004) *(3)*

6. Where the family go on holiday, leaving Kevin behind *(5)*

7. Clark gets stuck in this while hiding presents in *National Lampoon's Christmas Vacation* (1989) *(5)*

8. The person who is asked 'So how autobiographical is your work, Salman?' in *Bridget Jones's Diary* (2001) *(7)*

15. *Love Actually*'s Juliet (Keira Knightley) wants this from Mark *(5)*

16. 'Cheer Up, It's Christmas', a song by Wiley in this genre *(5)*

20. The counter in Bloomingdale's where *Serendipity*'s (2001) lead characters meet *(5)*

21. *Curious George: A Very ___ Christmas* (2009) (hint: it's an animal) *(6)*

22. Interchangeable with Dec for Billy Mack *(3)*

24. Every time a bell rings, what gets his wings? *(5)*

25. Who did Shakin' Stevens want to wish 'Merry Christmas' to? *(8)*

27. Seth Rogen's character attends this while high at midnight in *The Night Before* (2015) *(4)*

28. Experience Christmas at Hogwarts at the Harry Potter Studio ___ in Watford *(4)*

29. They told us 'IT'S CHRIIIIISTMAAAAS!' *(5)*

32. A Merry Christmas is wished to you and your – what? *(3)*

34. Pentatonix repeatedly ask her if she knew *(4)*

35. *Rock n' ___ Christmas* (2019) *(4)*

37. Amy March falls through it *(3)*

39. The gun Ralphie in *A Christmas Story* (1983) wants for Christmas *(2)*

40. What happened *on 5th Avenue* in 1947? *(2)*

41. *Marley* broke Christmas Day records when it was released in 2008, with whom? *(2)*

(See page 202 for the answers.)

FESTIVE WORDSEARCHES

Stars of Christmas Films

BRUCE WILLIS	HUGH GRANT	BILL MURRAY
WILL FERRELL	KATE WINSLET	JUDY GARLAND
TIM ALLEN	EMILIA CLARKE	VANESSA HUDGENS
JAMES STEWART	KRISTEN BELL	EDDIE MURPHY
JIM CARREY	MARTIN FREEMAN	

```
E Z T I M A L L E N B D P C V C X J L E
K B Q L A I W I X M T X D P T B I T P Y
R T F G C D R B I L L M U R R A Y P K H
A S I L L I W E C U R B A E Q T P X A P
L Z Z V K F P Y H M P W G B A D M J T R
C J I M C A R R E Y E P M S I P H T E U
A M D K N V U W Z T Z E U N V W N U W M
I A M B E L H J S H H B G E Z C T T I E
L D A J H C Z S J L P P D G W K M N N I
I N R M S S E L R L K E C D J M D A S D
M A T E S M B A O E R M F U H D V R L D
E L I Z A N T F E R I Y B H G S N G E E
Q R N J X U R K H R S G X A V S X H T Y
Q A F Q O Z H U X E T E G S S V X G J G
G G R B T A Q Z J F E P G S J J H U O V
X Y E H I O X B Q L N H O E R E X H H O
R D E N C Q V N K L B R J N C H O T V L
D U M R P Y V Q S I E Y T A T Z U P I U
X J A A V K D A F W L C A V H H L U B T
F Y N R I F I P C W L R F R E T W F H U
```

(See page 203 for the answers.)

FESTIVE WORDSEARCHES

TV That's Popular at Christmas

TOP OF THE POPS	EASTENDERS	QUEENS SPEECH
CORONATION STREET	DELIA SMITH	CAROLS FROM KINGS
STRICTLY COME DANCING	DOCTOR WHO	BAKE OFF
CALL THE MIDWIFE	ESSEXMAS	THE TWO RONNIES
ONLY FOOLS AND HORSES	BIG FAT QUIZ	VICAR OF DIBLEY

```
M Z Z U B A K E O F F I A V V L U Q Q V
T U U A K O V A X P X D W D A Q T Q V L
H N N V B H P E Z H F V G B K S S U O O
E K S P O P E H T F O P O T H R A B A H
T V E U C N H J L Y J E R A E Z Q Y S W
W S B I G F A T Q U I Z R D Z V R O D R
O G A C O R O N A T I O N S T R E E T O
R N J M S B H O O P K E K E I N H T T T
O I W I G U U J S T T L R V O Z Q N Z C
N K G O E J R N V S K D Z Y G U O Z X O
N M C Y A C D B A D E L I A S M I T H D
I O J R M R S E B J Q J G R S N W Q L E
E R Z I Q U E E N S S P E E C H W D Y Y
S F O N L Y F O O L S A N D H O R S E S
N S T R I C T L Y C O M E D A N C I N G
T L V I C A R O F D I B L E Y M Z O I I
V O W H P C H Z A A Y R D Q A Y V J K P
E R P J M X T V R N F S A M X E S S E A
C A L L T H E M I D W I F E X T X P S C
C C I O G Y P T Y Z T N Y H K I I Y F W
```

(See page 204 for the answers.)

173

Artists Who Made Christmas Songs

SLADE	WHAM	POGUES	WIZZARD
CLIFF RICHARD	MARIAH CAREY	BONEY M	BEACH BOYS
LEONA LEWIS	ELVIS	JONA LEWIE	JUSTIN BIEBER

```
L X O Y H N R U D J H X Y D G T Q R Y Z
D E E I W E L A N O J W C X Y Y E S C B
L X H P E R D I Y V S E K R Q Q I P B H
F D W T J I P O U O F Q U D Y G K P B W
X J G V I O M S F M V H U Y Z I F U Y Z
X C S O G J D R S Y B E A C H B O Y S U
N B T U E X X J U E R Y A G P I K Z P X
Q G E I W O W M P N U R F B J R Z W L N
A S U U F O D H Q O Q C E N Y U W I E J
S I V L E I R N G B L E N Y V S F W O U
D R A H C I R F F I L C F S L A D E N S
C X Z W Y M G G K Q B S O A N P X T A T
U G M M A R I A H C A R E Y Y S D J L I
S W V K B W G G Q Y I R Z R J Y G N E N
C P T P P K I A A I V I U A O S E A W B
E U G R Q M S Z C U S C P P X F P P I I
E G O T Q R X X Z B M X D X Y F M L S E
Q I J R W D T S F A B C O Z N A U J Q B
Z S C J B I X L F J R N H G H N G H L E
C J T E H G Y H D F R D Q W W I R J R R
```

(See page 205 for the answers.)

FESTIVE WORDSEARCHES

Foods You Only Eat at Christmas

BRANDY BUTTER	STILTON	TURKEY	SPOUTS
CHRISTMAS PUDDING	STOLLEN	MINCE PIES	TRIFLE
CRANBERRY SAUCE	EGGNOG	YULE LOG	PARSNIPS
MULLED WINE			

```
J O T K N O Z S Z O R A E I A Z Q F E G
E M P A J H X A N F S P R O U T S N C N
A R B K P A Q Z T J U N Q P U Y X O U I
Y E K R U T N E L L O T S R F D B T A D
A T A G W Y R F L J I V Z X Q E R L S D
I K B R A N D Y B U T T E R Y W Z I Y U
P G A D O A J H A S Y Z C U U G G T R P
P X I Q T Q B H W F H W M J L Y M S R S
A S F D O E E X T D Z L K O E H P Q E A
R Y K J L D U H X J N P Q N L B M T B M
S A R R L X W H T Y I E Y X O Y E G N T
N U Q X S Z A B E R N Y L K G G E K A S
I Y D F Y P H Y V S Z E K F G F F M R I
P W P M I N C E P I E S C N I U O A C R
S M G W V R Y Q U H Q G O H L R X Z M H
G C E E B C D A V M J G G L W O T W L C
L K E I L H O L Q S C A I Q N G J Z N F
G H M F F C H E B Y U F J L M L D W F A
E M U N T W M U L L E D W I N E F Q U U
H V B L H U N R W J P H J K A R X X L K
```

(See page 206 for the answers.)

SONGS IN CODE

Can you decode these titles of classic Christmas tunes?

1. Circumnavigate the fir while headbanging
2. Every staunch believer, approach
3. Zero noise between sundown and dawn
4. Mature, benevolent monarch
5. Delight directed towards globe
6. Us rulers numbering one more than two
7. On a transparent witching hour it arrived

8. Slight male percussionist
9. My maternal parent was spied by myself committing adultery
10. Chimes of semi-precious metals
11. Let the foyers be festooned
12. Rambling in awe across some cold earth
13. *Ilex aquifolium* and *Hedera helix*
14. Hoofed ruminant mammal with rouged facial protuberance
15. Pay attention to the warbling cherubs announcing something
16. Petite ass

(See page 207 for the answers.)

JINGLE ALL THE WAY

Match the song to the Christmas advert

'Silent Night'	John Lewis ad, in which a snowman searches for the ideal gift for his love
'Magic Moments'	Irn-Bru ad, in which a snowman nicks a boy's drink
'Somewhere Only We Know'	M&S ad, in which people put on jumpers and find they can't help but dance
'Wonderful Dream (Holidays Are Coming)'	John Lewis ad, in which Buster the Boxer has a great time on a trampoline
'Walking in the Air' (adapted lyrics)	John Lewis ad, in which a boy excitedly anticipates Christmas so he can give his parents their present
'The Power of Love'	Coca-Cola ad, in which a holiday Coca-Cola truck brings joy to all
'One Day I'll Fly Away'	Sainsbury's '1914' ad, in which soldiers from the trenches play football together
'Jump Around'	Quality Street ad, in which a boy gives his lollipop lady a gift of chocolates
'Please, Please, Please, Let Me Get What I Want'	Boots ad, in which ladies get ready for a night out
'Here Come the Girls'	John Lewis ad, in which a hare gifts a hibernating bear an alarm clock so he doesn't miss Christmas

(See page 208 for the answers.)

O COME AND FILL IN
THE BLANKS!

How hot are you on your Christmas carols? Do you know your 'O Come, All Ye Faithful' from your 'O Come, O Come, Emmanuel'? Your 'Silent Night' from your 'O Holy Night'? Could you navigate your way through Royal David's City and come out in Bethlehem?

If so, why not have a go at filling in the gaps in the verses below, as well as identifying which carol they're taken from. Give yourself a point for every title and missing word you identify. And if you score as highly as the lady is favoured, why not challenge someone to beat your score?

1. Title: _____

    'The ____ are lowing
    The baby awakes
    But little Lord Jesus
    No ____ He makes'

2. Title: _____

   '_____ night, holy night!
   _____ quake at the sight
   Glories stream from heaven afar
   Heavenly hosts sing _____!'

3. Title: _____

   'Good _____ Wenceslas looked out
   On the _____ of Stephen
   When the snow lay round about
   _____ and crisp and even'

4. Title: _____

   'Hail! the heaven-born
   _____ of peace!
   Hail! the Son of Righteousness!
   Light and _____ to all he brings,
   Risen with healing in his _____'

5. Title: _____

   'For Christ is born of Mary
   And gathered all above
   While _____ sleep, the _____ keep
   Their watch of wondering love'

6. Title: _____

'Born a King on _____'s plain
Gold I bring to crown Him again
King for ever, ceasing never
Over us all to ____'

7. Title: _____

'In the bleak _____, frosty wind made moan,
Earth stood _____ as iron, water like a _____;
Snow had fallen, snow on _____, snow on _____,
In the bleak _____, long ago'

8. Title: _____

'The holly bears a prickle
As sharp as any ____
And Mary bore sweet Jesus Christ
On Christmas _____ in the morn'

(See page 208 for the answers.)

IT'S A WONDERFUL RIDDLE: THE LOGIC OF THE CHRISTMAS MOVIE

1. What is seen at the beginning of *A Christmas Story* and at the end of *Bad Santa* but never in *Gremlins*?

_____

2. You are Kevin McCallister and you have three air-guns. If you take two away, how many do you have?

_____

3. A girl is going to visit Kris Kringle at Cole's Department Store, and she wants to ask for a remote-control car, as well as a gift for each of her siblings. She has as many brothers as sisters, but each brother has only half as

many brothers as sisters. How many presents does she need to ask for in total?

_____

4. In *The Family Stone,* Meredith (Sarah Jessica Parker) comes to stay in her fiancés family home for Christmas. She goes poking around the house and finds something that goes up and down but doesn't move. What is it?

_____

5. You are staying in the lovely cottage owned by Iris (Kate Winslet) in *The Holiday,* and you have a power cut. You find a kerosene lamp, a candle and a fireplace. What do you light first?

_____

6. In *'Twas the Night Before Christmas* (1974), what has hands but can't clap?

_____

7. In *Elf,* what has words but never speaks?

_____

8. Amy, Kiki and Carla are having a stressful time in *A Bad Moms Christmas*. Amy is looking at Kiki. Kiki is looking at Carla. Amy is drunk, Kiki isn't, and we don't know if Carla is. Is a drunk person looking at a sober person?

_____

9. The Grinch discovers that the day before two days after the day before tomorrow is Christmas Day. So what day is it today?

_____

10. What is heavier: a ton of candy cane (such as Buddy the Elf would eat for breakfast) or a ton of snow (such as that falling in Vermont in the final scene of *White Christmas*)?

_____

11. The Snowman is flying over an ocean on the way to the North Pole. Beneath him he sees a boat filled with people. But when he looks again, it hasn't sunk or capsized and yet there's not a single person on it. Why is that?

_____

12. It's the dress rehearsal in *Nativity!* but lots of the kids are running late. So far all except two of the kids present are from the sound team, all except two are in the cast, and all except two are backstage crew. How many kids are present for rehearsal?

_____

(See page 208 for the answers.)

CHAPTER 5
ANSWERS

1. It's Beginning to Look a Lot Like Quizmas

ROCKIN' ROBIN: MUSIC
ROUND 1
Official Christmas Number Ones

1. The Beatles
2. Nicole Kidman
3. 'Mistletoe and Wine'
4. 'I Love Sausage Rolls' by LadBaby
5. George Michael
6. 'Mr Blobby'
7. 'Lonely This Christmas' by Mud (1974)
8. Shayne Ward
9. The Spice Girls
10. Harry Belafonte
11. Twelve
12. Christ Church Cathedral Choir, Oxford
13. 'Perfect'
14. Rage Against the Machine
15. Queen with 'Bohemian Rhapsody'

ROUND 2
Favourite Christmas Hits

1. Bing Crosby
2. Britney Spears
3. 'Santa Baby'
4. 'The Christmas Song'
5. José Feliciano

6. 'White Christmas' (1942)
7. Justin Bieber
8. The Tweenies
9. Kelly Clarkson
10. A pair of Chloé shades and a diamond belly ring
11. 1988
12. 'Wonderful Christmastime'
13. (Don't Let the Bells End)
14. Wales
15. 'Can't Smile Without You'

ROUND 3
Songs from the Movies

1. 'Let It Snow! Let It Snow! Let It Snow!'
2. 'Santa Claus Is Comin' to Town'
3. 'Have Yourself a Merry Little Christmas'
4. *Scrooged* (1988)
5. 'One More Sleep 'til Christmas'
6. 'Good King Wenceslas'
7. Leon Jackson
8. 'What's This?'
9. 'Jingle Bell Rock'
10. *The Best Little Whorehouse in Texas* (1982)
11. *Home Alone* (1990)
12. *Holiday Inn* (1942)
13. 'Santa's Super Sleigh'
14. *It's a Wonderful Life* (1946)
15. 'Do You Hear What I Hear?'

ROUND 4
Christmas Carols

1. Ukrainian
2. Three
3. Gathering firewood
4. 1818
5. 'In the Bleak Midwinter'
6. 'What Child Is This?'
7. Slay all the babies
8. Thanksgiving
9. The Cuban Missile Crisis
10. 'Little Donkey'
11. Martin Luther
12. 'Silent Night'
13. Three Dog Night
14. 'It Came Upon the Midnight Clear'
15. 'O Come, O Come, Emmanuel'

ROUND 5
Guess the Song from the Lyric

1. 'I Saw Mommy Kissing Santa Claus'
2. 'Last Christmas'
3. 'All I Want for Christmas Is You'
4. 'Run Rudolph Run'
5. 'O Holy Night'
6. *'Feliz Navidad'*
7. 'Driving Home for Christmas'
8. 'God Rest Ye Merry, Gentlemen'

9. 'A Holly Jolly Christmas'
10. 'Have Yourself a Merry Little Christmas'
11. 'Santa Baby'
12. 'Rockin' Around the Christmas Tree'
13. 'Stop the Cavalry'
14. 'Mistletoe'
15. 'My Only Wish'
16. 'The Holly and the Ivy'
17. 'I Wish It Could Be Christmas Everyday'
18. 'While Shepherds Watched Their Flocks'
19. 'Lonely This Christmas'
20. 'It's Beginning to Look a Lot Like Christmas'

ROUND 6
Find the Link

1. 'The Holly and the Ivy' (Sun, Deer, Crown, Ivy, Holly)
2. 'The Christmas Song' aka 'Chestnuts Roasting on an Open Fire' (Fire, Carols, *Jack Frost*, Nose, Chestnut)
3. 'The Twelve Days of Christmas' (Rings, Piper, Drummers, Goose, Maid)
4. 'Jingle Bells' (Dash, Snow, Horse, *Slay* [Sleigh], Bells)

ROCKIN' ROBIN: PICTURE ROUND
Dingbats Merrily on High

1. 'Rockin' Around the Christmas Tree'
2. 'The First Noel'
3. 'Walking in the Air'
4. 'Last Christmas'

5. 'Walking in a Winter Wonderland'
6. 'Christmas Time'
7. 'All I Want for Christmas Is You'
8. 'Away in a Manger'
9. 'Santa Baby'
10. 'The Little Drummer Boy'
11. '8 Days of Christmas'
12. 'Step Into Christmas'

Match the Artist to the Song

'Christmas in Harlem'	–	Kanye West
'Please Come Home for Christmas'	–	Bon Jovi
'Wit It This Christmas'	–	Ariana Grande
'I Saw Mommy Kissing Santa Claus'	–	The Jackson 5
'Step Into Christmas'	–	Elton John
'Underneath the Tree'	–	Kelly Clarkson
'One More Sleep'	–	Leona Lewis
'My Sad Christmas Song'	–	Miley Cyrus

Festive Movie Scramble!

LITTLE DONKEY

MARY'S BOY CHILD

FAIRYTALE OF NEWYORK

JINGLE BELL ROCK

CHAPTER 5: ANSWERS

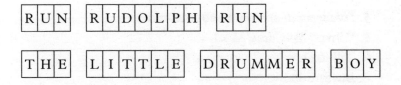

RUN RUDOLPH RUN

THE LITTLE DRUMMER BOY

ROCKIN' ROBIN: FOR KIDS (AND BIG KIDS)
Festive Music Quiz

1. Lords a-leaping
2. 'O Christmas Tree'
3. Thirty-two
4. Play games
5. A button
6. In his sack
7. The cows mooing
8. Under the mistletoe
9. 'Happy Christmas to all, and to all a good night!'
10. Twice
11. Parson Brown
12. Boughs of holly
13. Rudolph the Red-nosed Reindeer
14. That they have some
15. A precious load

QUIZ ACTUALLY: MOVIES
ROUND 1
Early Classics

1. *The Shop Around the Corner*
2. Natalie Wood
3. 'For Me and My Gal'

4. *It Happened on 5th Avenue* (1947)
5. 'Thank You Very Much'
6. The Bishop's
7. Bedford Falls
8. Irving Berlin
9. *Diamonds Are Forever*
10. *3 Godfathers*
11. Their army general from the war
12. A former employee in the poor house
13. 1898
14. *Black Christmas*
15. *It's a Wonderful Life* (1946)

ROUND 2

The Golden Age – a Millennial's Childhood

1. *Home Alone* (1990)
2. Zero
3. *Home Alone 2: Lost in New York* (1992)
4. Now I have a machine gun. HO - HO - HO
5. Michael Caine
6. $1
7. Chris Columbus
8. He falls off the roof
9. Turbo-Man
10. Trainers
11. Mount Crumpit
12. A taxi driver
13. Cole's
14. The Sticky Bandits
15. *You've Got Mail* (1998)

CHAPTER 5: ANSWERS

ROUND 3
A More Modern Christmas

1. *A Christmas Prince* (2017)
2. Syrup
3. Cry
4. A reindeer
5. Four
6. The Nutcracker Ball
7. Vince Vaughn
8. Wandsworth
9. Mushrooms
10. Jada Pinkett Smith
11. A pink elephant
12. Alanis Morissette
13. Greg Wise
14. Five
15. *Love Actually*

ROUND 4
Critics' Reviews: Identify the Film

1. *Home Alone* (1990)
2. *Jingle All the Way* (1996)
3. *How the Grinch Stole Christmas* (2000)
4. *Miracle on 34th Street* (1994)
5. *Elf* (2003)
6. *Office Christmas Party* (2016)
7. *A Muppet Christmas Carol* (1992)
8. *Love Actually* (2003)
9. *The Holiday* (2006)

10. *The Santa Clause* (1994)
11. *It's a Wonderful Life* (1946)
12. *Last Christmas* (2019)
13. *Gremlins* (1984)
14. *Bad Santa* (2003)
15. *Nativity!* (2009)

ROUND 5
Guess the Film from One Quote

1. *It's a Wonderful Life* (1946)
2. *Love Actually* (2003)
3. *Elf* (2003)
4. *Home Alone* (1990)
5. *The Nightmare Before Christmas* (1993)
6. *Miracle on 34th Street* (1994)
7. *Jingle All the Way* (1996)
8. *White Christmas* (1954)
9. *How the Grinch Stole Christmas* (2000)
10. *The Muppet Christmas Carol* (1992)
11. *Miracle on 34th Street* (1947)
12. *A Charlie Brown Christmas* (1965)
13. *Scrooged* (1988)
14. *Home Alone 2: Lost in New York* (1992)
15. *Arthur Christmas* (2011)

ROUND 6
Find the Link

1. *The Holiday* (Beach, Bag, Son [Sun], Plane, Passport)
2. *Nativity!* (Inn, Wise, Gold, Star, Donkey)

3. *Love Actually* (Rowan Atkinson, Martin Freeman, Emma Thompson, Martine McCutcheon, Liam Neeson)
4. *Frozen* (Ice, Reindeer, Magic, Queen, freezing point)

QUIZ ACTUALLY: PICTURE ROUND
Dingbats Merrily on High

1. *White Christmas* (1954)
2. *Noel,* i.e. No L (2004)
3. *The Shop Around the Corner* (1940)
4. *Just Friends* (2005)
5. *Home Alone* (1990)
6. *Four Christmases* (2008)
7. *Little Women* (2019)
8. *Die Hard* (1988)
9. *A Christmas Carol* (2009)
10. *The Princess Switch* (2018)
11. *The Santa Clause* (1994)
12. *Krampus* (2015)

Blink and You'd Miss Them!

Ant and Dec	–	*Love Actually*
Steven Tyler (Aerosmith)	–	*The Polar Express*
Alan Carr	–	*Nativity!*
Mindy Kaling	–	*The Night Before*
Dustin Hoffman	–	*The Holiday*
Sue Perkins	–	*Last Christmas*
Peter Dinklage	–	*Elf*
John Candy	–	*Home Alone*

Festive Movie Scramble!

THE SNOWMAN

DIE HARD

CHRISTMAS WITH THE KRANKS

BAD SANTA

THE HOLIDAY

SCROOGE

QUIZ ACTUALLY: FOR KIDS

Festive Movie Quiz

1. Olaf
2. Hot chocolate
3. A hovercraft
4. Green
5. Halloween Town
6. Mr Poppy
7. The key to her mother's music box
8. A mammoth
9. A scarf
10. Three
11. HO HO HO
12. A puppy
13. The Family Tree
14. Gold, frankincense and myrrh
15. Cindy Lou Who

4. HOME ALONE? PUZZLES TO KEEP YOU ENTERTAINED

JOLLYWORD PUZZLES

1.

1	2	3	4	5	6	7	8	9	10	11	12	13	14	15	16
							1W	I	T	**2**H					
										H	**3**O				
4H		**5**J	O	Y		**6**B	E	L	I	E	V	E	**7**C		
8A	V	E		**9**M		L				E			H		
N		**10**S	A	V	I	O	U	R		**11**P	R	O	P	E	R
K		U		S		E		**12**U		O				E	
E		**13**S	A	N	T	A		**14**N	E	W	Y	O	R	K	
Y				L	**16**N			D		E	N			Y	
	17D	A	N	C	E			I		E	R		E		
	O			T				C		R		**18**S		**19**M	
20O	N	E		**21**R	O	C	K	I	N		**22**T	E	E	T	H / **23**H
K		**24**X		E				E		A			R		O
E		M		**25**C	**26**A	V	A	L	**27**R	Y			R		M
28Y	E	A	R		I			T		U			Y		E
		S			R			H		N					

2.

¹S	E	R	E	N	²D	³I	⁴T	Y	⁵A	⁶S
N					I	O	O		⁷R	O	C	K	Y
⁸O	F	F	⁹I	C	E		L	Y	R		R
W			N		¹⁰H	A	L	L	S	O	O
¹¹M	E	¹²A	N			R	A		U	O
A		C	¹³A	¹⁴S		¹⁵S	N	O	W	¹⁶D	O	G
¹⁷N	A	T	I	V	I	T	Y	D	O	¹⁸E	L	¹⁹F
	U		E		O		M	D	R
	A		N		N		E	E
²⁰C	L	A	U	S	E	²¹K	R	A	N	K	²²S	D
²³S		L		E		N		T
²⁴W	H	Y	²⁵H	O	L	I	D	A	Y	R
I		A		G		²⁶B	E	A	²⁷S	T
²⁸T	O	²⁹M	L		³⁰H	³¹W		E	T	H
C		O	³²L	A	S	T	A	³³S	T	O	L	E
³⁴H	O	M	E	S			Y

3.

The completed crossword grid:

¹S	C	²H	W	³A	R	Z	E	N	⁴E	⁵G	G	E	⁶R
T	■	O	■	C	■	■	■	■	I	R	■	■	E
O	■	M	■	⁷O	R	G	A	N	N	⁸I	R	I	S
⁹C	H	E	E	R	■	■	■	■	S	N	■	■	T
K	■	S	■	¹⁰N	¹¹I	G	H	T	T	¹²C	C	¹³T	■
I	■	■	M	■	■	I	■	■	E	H	H	H	■
¹⁴N	U	T	C	R	A	C	K	E	R	■	¹⁶B	E	T
G	¹⁵E	E	■	G	■	G	■	S	■	■	K	■	■
¹⁷S	O	N	■	■	¹⁸I	E	■	C	■	¹⁹H	A	I	L
■	■	²⁰L	I	N	C	O	L	N	²¹N	N	■	■	L
²²B	■	■	A	■	E	■	A	■	E	■	■	²³L	A
²⁴A	B	O	U	T	■	■	■	L	■	²⁵W	I	N	E
K	■	R	■	■	²⁶P	■	■	Y	■	■	R	■	■
E	²⁷J	I	N	G	L	E	B	E	L	L	S	■	■
R	■	E	■	■	U	■	■	A	■	■	■	■	■
²⁸Y	E	S	■	²⁹A	R	M	S	T	R	O	N	G	■

4.

Crossword grid (across answers read by row; ■ = shaded square):

Row 1: ¹L O S ²A N ³G E ⁴L E ⁵S ■ ⁶P ■ ⁷A I ⁸R
Row 2: E ■ R ■ R ■ U ■ ⁹I N F A N T ■ U
Row 3: ¹⁰O G R E ■ R E ¹¹M A X ■ R T ■ ■ S
Row 4: N ■ N ■ M ■ O ■ ¹²I R I S H
Row 5: ¹³A L E D ■ ¹⁴L A ¹⁵S V ¹⁶E G A S ■ C ¹⁷A D
Row 6: L ■ E ■ I ■ I ■ I R ■ A I
Row 7: ¹⁸E N G L A N D ■ ¹⁹D R I V I N G ²⁰G E
Row 8: W ■ L ■ S ■ E ■ M ■ L
Row 9: I ■ E ■ ²¹M O O R E ²²A B O V E
Row 10: ²³S I ²⁴A ²⁵E O ■ A N V
Row 11: N ²⁶V E N T ²⁷M A ²⁸T T H E W ²⁹S
Row 12: ³⁰E A G L E K A O L
Row 13: E E R E ³¹S T U C K ³²K ³³H A
Row 14: ³⁴M I L E Y C Y ³⁵R U S R I D
Row 15: A O O ³⁶N ³⁷I C E
Row 16: ³⁸R ³⁹O B I N W I ⁴⁰L L ⁴¹I A M S C
Row 17: Y B E L T E ⁴²B E A R

FESTIVE WORDSEARCHES
Stars of Christmas Films

```
E Z T I M A L L E N B D P C V C X J L E
K B Q L A I W I X M T X D P T B I T P Y
R T F G C D R B I L L M U R R A Y P K H
A S I L L I W E C U R B A E Q T P X A P
L Z Z V K F P Y H M P W G B A D M J T R
C J I M C A R R E Y E P M S I P H T E U
A M D K N V U W Z T E U N V W N U W M
I A M B E L H J S H H B G E Z C T T I E
L D A J H C Z S J L P P D G W K M N N I
I N R M S S E L R L K E C D J M D A S D
M A T E S M B A O E R M F U H D V R L D
E L I Z A N T F E R I Y B H G S N G E E
Q R N J X U R K H R S G X A V S X H T Y
Q A F Q O Z H U X E T E G S S V X G J G
G G R B T A Q Z J F E P G S J J H U O V
X Y E H I O X B Q L N H O E R E X H H O
R D E N C Q V N K L B R J N C H O T V L
D U M R P Y V Q S I E Y T A T Z U P I U
X J A A V K D A F W L C A V H H L U B T
F Y N R I F I P C W L R F R E T W F H U
```

TV That's Popular at Christmas

```
M Z Z U B A K E O F F I A V V L U Q Q V
T U U A K O V A X P X D W D A Q T Q V L
H N N V B H P E Z H F V G B K S S U O O
E K S P O P E H T F O P O T H R A B A H
T V E U C N H J L Y J E R A E Z Q Y S W
W S B I G F A T Q U I Z R D Z V R O D R
O G A C O R O N A T I O N S T R E E T O
R N J M S B H O O P K E K E I N H T T T
O I W I G U U J S T T L R V O Z Q N Z C
N K G O E J R N V S K D Z Y G U O Z X O
N M C Y A C D B A D E L I A S M I T H D
I O J R M R S E B J Q J G R S N W Q L E
E R Z I Q U E E N S S P E E C H W D Y Y
S F O N L Y F O O L S A N D H O R S E S
N S T R I C T L Y C O M E D A N C I N G
T L V I C A R O F D I B L E Y M Z O I I
V O W H P C H Z A A Y R D Q A Y V J K P
E R P J M X T V R N F S A M X E S S E A
C A L L T H E M I D W I F E X T X P S C
C C I O G Y P T Y Z T N Y H K I I Y F W
```

Artists Who Made Christmas Songs

```
L X O Y H N R U D J H X Y D G T Q R Y Z
D E E I W E L A N O J W C X Y Y E S C B
L X H P E R D I Y V S E K R Q Q I P B H
F D W T J I P O U O F Q U D Y G K P B W
X J G V I O M S F M V H U Y Z I F U Y Z
X C S O G J D R S Y B E A C H B O Y S U
N B T U E X X J U E R Y A G P I K Z P X
Q G E I W O W M P N U R F B J R Z W L N
A S U U F O D H Q O Q C E N Y U W I E J
S I V L E I R N G B L E N Y V S F W O U
D R A H C I R F F I L C F S L A D E N S
C X Z W Y M G G K Q B S O A N P X T A T
U G M M A R I A H C A R E Y Y S D J L I
S W V K B W G G Q Y I R Z R J Y G N E N
C P T P P K I A A I V I U A O S E A W B
E U G R Q M S Z C U S C P P X F P P I I
E G O T Q R X X Z B M X D X Y F M L S E
Q I J R W D T S F A B C O Z N A U J Q B
Z S C J B I X L F J R N H G H N G H L E
C J T E H G Y H D F R D Q W W I R J R R
```

Food You Only Eat at Christmas

```
J O T K N O Z S Z O R A E I A Z Q F E G
E M P A J H X A N F S P R O U T S N C N
A R B K P A Q Z T J U N Q P U Y X O U I
Y E K R U T N E L L O T S R F D B T A D
A T A G W Y R F L J I V Z X Q E R L S D
I K B R A N D Y B U T T E R Y W Z I Y U
P G A D O A J H A S Y Z C U U G G T R P
P X I Q T Q B H W F H W M J L Y M S R S
A S F D O E E X T D Z L K O E H P Q E A
R Y K J L D U H X J N P Q N L B M T B M
S A R R L X W H T Y I E Y X O Y E G N T
N U Q X S Z A B E R N Y L K G G E K A S
I Y D F Y P H Y V S Z E K F G F F M R I
P W P M I N C E P I E S C N I U O A C R
S M G W V R Y Q U H Q G O H L R X Z M H
G C E E B C D A V M J G G L W O T W L C
L K E I L H O L Q S C A I Q N G J Z N F
G H M F F C H E B Y U F J L M L D W F A
E M U N T W M U L L E D W I N E F Q U U
H V B L H U N R W J P H J K A R X X L K
```

CHAPTER 5: ANSWERS

SONGS IN CODE

1. 'Rockin' Around the Christmas Tree'
2. 'O Come, All Ye Faithful'
3. 'Silent Night'
4. 'Good King Wenceslas'
5. 'Joy to the World'
6. 'We Three Kings'
7. 'It Came Upon a Midnight Clear'
8. 'The Little Drummer Boy'
9. 'I Saw Mommy Kissing Santa Claus'
10. 'Silver Bells'
11. 'Deck the Halls'
12. 'Winter Wonderland'
13. 'The Holly and the Ivy'
14. 'Rudolph the Red-nosed Reindeer'
15. 'Hark! The Herald Angels Sing'
16. 'Little Donkey'

JINGLE ALL THE WAY

'Silent Night'	Sainsbury's '1914' ad, in which soldiers from the trenches play football together
'Magic Moments'	Quality Street ad, in which a boy gives his lollipop lady a gift of chocolates
'Somewhere Only We Know'	John Lewis ad, in which a hare gifts a hibernating bear an alarm clock so he doesn't miss Christmas
'Wonderful Dream (Holidays Are Coming)'	Coca-Cola ad, in which a holiday Coca-Cola truck brings joy to all
'Walking in the Air' (adapted lyrics)	Irn-Bru ad, in which a snowman nicks a boy's drink
'The Power of Love'	John Lewis ad, in which a snowman searches for the ideal gift for his love

'One Day I'll Fly Away'	John Lewis ad, in which Buster the Boxer has a great time on a trampoline
'Jump Around'	M&S ad, in which people put on jumpers and find they can't help but dance
'Please, Please, Please, Let Me Get What I Want'	John Lewis ad, in which a boy excitedly anticipates Christmas so he can give his parents a present
'Here Come the Girls'	Boots ad, in which ladies get ready for a night out

O COME AND FILL IN THE BLANKS

1. 'Away in a Manger' – cattle; crying
2. 'Silent Night' – Silent; Shepherds; Alleluia
3. 'Good King Wenceslas' – King; Feast; Deep
4. 'Hark! The Herald Angels Sing' – Prince; life; wings
5. 'O Little Town of Bethlehem' – mortals; angels
6. 'We Three Kings' – Bethlehem; reign
7. 'In the Bleak Midwinter' – midwinter; hard; stone; snow; snow; midwinter
8. 'The Holly and the Ivy' – thorn; Day

IT'S A WONDERFUL RIDDLE

1. The letter A.
2. You have the two you took away.
3. Seven – in her family there are four girls and three boys.
4. A staircase.
5. A match.
6. A clock.

7. A book.
8. Yes. If Carla is drunk, then she is drunk and looking at Kiki, who is sober. If Carla is sober, then Amy, who is drunk, is looking at her. Either way, the statement is correct.
9. Christmas Eve. The 'day before tomorrow' is today, 'the day before two days after' actually just means one day after. So if one day after today is Christmas Day, today must be Christmas Eve! He had better hop to it.
10. They're both a ton, so equally heavy.
11. They're all married.
12. There are three kids. One from sound, one from the cast and one from backstage.

CREDITS

Rockin' Robin: Round 5

1. 'I Saw Mommy Kissing Santa Claus' by The Jackson 5, written by Tommie Connor
2. 'Last Christmas' by Wham!, written by George Michael
3. 'All I Want for Christmas Is You' by Mariah Carey, written by Mariah Carey and Walter Afanasieff
4. 'Run Rudolph Run' by Chuck Berry, written by Johnny Marks and Marvin Brodie
5. 'O Holy Night', written by Adolphe Adam
6. *'Feliz Navidad'* by José Feliciano, written by José Feliciano
7. 'Driving Home for Christmas' by Chris Rea, written by Chris Rea
8. 'God Rest Ye Merry, Gentlemen', traditional, writer unknown
9. 'A Holly Jolly Christmas' by Burl Ives, written by Johnny Marks
10. 'Have Yourself a Merry Little Christmas' by Judy Garland, written by Hugh Martin and Ralph Blane

CREDITS

11. 'Santa Baby' by Eartha Kitt, written by Joan Javits and Philip Springer
12. 'Rockin' Around the Christmas Tree' by Brenda Lee, written by Johnny Marks
13. 'Stop the Cavalry' by Jona Lewie, written by Jona Lewie
14. 'Mistletoe' by Justin Bieber, written by Nasri and Adam Messinger
15. 'My Only Wish' by Britney Spears, written by Britney Spears, Brian Kierulf and Josh Schwartz
16. 'The Holly and the Ivy', traditional, writer unknown
17. 'I Wish It Could Be Christmas Everyday' by Wizzard, written by Roy Wood
18. 'While Shepherds Watched Their Flocks', written by Nahum Tate
19. 'Lonely This Christmas' by Mud, written by Nicky Chinn and Mike Chapman
20. 'It's Beginning to Look a Lot Like Christmas' by Perry Como and The Fontane Sisters, written by Meredith Wilson

Rockin' Robin: Round 6

1. 'The Holly and the Ivy', traditional, writer unknown
2. 'The Christmas Song' by Nat King Cole, written by Bob Wells and Mel Tormé
3. 'The Twelve Days of Christmas', traditional, arranged by Frederic Austin
4. 'Jingle Bells' by Bing Crosby and The Andrews Sisters, written by James Lord Pierpont

Rockin' Robin: Picture Round

1. 'Rockin' Around the Christmas Tree' by Brenda Lee, written by Johnny Marks
2. 'The First Noel', traditional, arranged by John Stainer
3. 'Walking in the Air' by Aled Jones, written by Howard Blake
4. 'Last Christmas' by Wham!, written by George Michael
5. 'Walking in a Winter Wonderland' by Frank Sinatra, written by Felix Bernard and Richard Bernhard Smith
6. 'Christmas Time' by The Darkness, written by Justin Hawkins, Dan Hawkins, Frankie Poullain and Ed Graham
7. 'All I Want for Christmas Is You' by Mariah Carey, written by Mariah Carey and Walter Afanasieff
8. 'Away in a Manger', traditional, arranged by Jonathan Spilman
9. 'Santa Baby' by Eartha Kitt, written by Joan Javits and Philip Springer
10. 'The Little Drummer Boy' by David Bowie and Bing Crosby, written by Katherine Kennicott Davis
11. '8 Days of Christmas' by Destiny's Child, written by Beyoncé, Kelly Rowland and Errol McCalla, Jr
12. 'Step Into Christmas' by Elton John, written by Elton John and Bernie Taupin

Quiz Actually: Round 4

1. Jake Euker, *F5* (Wichita, KS), July 2004
2. Heather Boerner, *Common Sense Media*, December 2010

3. Lisa Alspector, *Chicago Reader*, 2008

4. Almar Haflidason, BBC.com, 2001

5. Peter Bradshaw, *Guardian*, 2003

6. Kevin Carr, *Fat Guys at the Movies*, 2016

7. Peter Bradshaw, *Guardian*, 2017

8. Mary Elizabeth Williams, Salon.com, 2013

9. Stella Papamichael, *Radio Times*, 2006

10. Charles Cassady Jr, *Common Sense Media*, 2005

11. Jack D. Grant, *Hollywood Reporter*, 1946

12. Wendy Ide, *Guardian*, 2019

13. Neil Smith, *Total Film*, 2012

14. Kevin Carr, *Fat Guys at the Movies*, 2003

15. Robert Hanks, *Independent*, 2009

Quiz Actually: Round 5

1. *It's a Wonderful Life* (1946) – Liberty Films
2. *Love Actually* (2003) – Universal Pictures, StudioCanal, Working Title Films, DNA Films
3. *Elf* (2003) – New Line Cinema, Guy Walks into a Bar Productions
4. *Home Alone* (1990) – Twentieth Century Fox, Hughes Entertainment
5. *The Nightmare Before Christmas* (1993) – Walt Disney Pictures, Skellington Productions Inc., Touchstone Pictures
6. *Miracle on 34th Street* (1994) – Twentieth Century Fox, Hughes Entertainment
7. *Jingle All the Way* (1996) – Twentieth Century Fox, 1492 Pictures
8. *White Christmas* (1954) – Paramount Pictures

9. *How the Grinch Stole Christmas* (2000) – Universal Pictures, Imagine Entertainment, LUNI Productions GmbH & Company KG
10. *The Muppet Christmas Carol* (1992) – Walt Disney Pictures, Jim Henson Productions
11. *Miracle on 34th Street* (1947) – Twentieth Century Fox
12. *A Charlie Brown Christmas* (1965) – Lee Mendelson Film Productions, Bill Melendez Productions, United Feature Syndicate (UFS)
13. *Scrooged* (1988) – Paramount Pictures, Mirage Productions
14. *Home Alone 2: Lost in New York* (1992) – Twentieth Century Fox, Hughes Entertainment
15. *Arthur Christmas* (2011) – Sony Pictures Animation, Aardman Animations, Columbia Pictures Corporation